MY SISTER
ST. THÉRÈSE

St. Thérèse of the Child Jesus (right) and her sister Celine on the Veiling Day of the latter, Sister Geneviève of the Holy Face, March 17, 1896.

MY SISTER
ST. THÉRÈSE

By

Sister Geneviève of the Holy Face
(Celine Martin)

Authorized Translation by
The Carmelite Sisters of New York of
CONSEILS ET SOUVENIRS

TAN BOOKS AND PUBLISHERS, INC.
Rockford, Illinois 61105

Nihil Obstat: Edward Gallen
                 Censor Deputatus

Imprimi Potest: ✠ John Carol
                 Archbishop of Dublin, Primate of Ireland
                 Dublin
                 February 2, 1959

Library of Congress Catalog No.: 97-60610

ISBN 0-89555-598-0

TAN BOOKS AND PUBLISHERS, INC.
P.O. Box 424
Rockford, Illinois 61105
1997

"In my childhood I often read the lives of the saints, and these stories used to inspire me and inflame my heart. . . . By this means, I caught a glimpse of the ideal of sanctity, and how often I used to day-dream about it! Yet I had never made any living contact with it, for in order to touch something, we must be very close to it. . . . At Carmel, however, I found in our dear little Sister Thérèse all that I had been searching for, and through her, all these desires were realized."

—Sister Geneviève of the Holy Face
(*See page xxi*)

CONTENTS

FOREWORD TO THE
ENGLISH TRANSLATION

THIS *Memoir* has been translated from the revised edition of the French *Conseils et Souvenirs*, published at Lisieux by Soeur Geneviève de la Sainte Face in 1951. The change of title and other minor adaptations in this English version have been made with the approval of Soeur Geneviève and the Carmel of Lisieux. The translation has, moreover, been brought into line with the recent French publication of the original *Histoire d'Une Ame*, a photostatic copy of Saint Thérèse's manuscript before its revision by Mère Agnès de Jesus.

Even before her canonization in 1925, it had become abundantly clear that the life and "mission" of Thérèse of Lisieux would become a favourite theme for spiritual writers, and that her teaching, because of its essential simplicity, would lay itself open to innumerable inter- pretations. The Carmel of Lisieux, therefore, at the initiative of the late Mère Agnès de Jésus, Thérèse's sister, published during the last half century various authoritative commentaries on the life and on the doctrine of the Saint. Such works have served the double purpose of clari- fying Saint Thérèse's teaching and of correcting many false impressions about her life and her

Little Way. By this means we have come into possession of *At the School of Saint Thérèse*, *The Spirit of Saint Thérèse*, *Novissima Verba*, *The Story of a Family*, and *The Collected Letters of Saint Thérèse*.

These valuable documentations of the Saint's thoughts and characteristics together with official publications containing excerpts from the Canonization Process have, it would seem, made the world familiar with the chief features of the moral physiognomy of this " greatest saint of modern times." This recently published *Memoir* of her sister, Céline, however, brings up a new picture of the Saint as seen through the eyes of one who had a unique place in her heart.

This latest document bears the seal of the supernatural under several titles. First, it comes to us from a venerable religious, Soeur Geneviève de la Sainte Face, who has spent more than sixty-three years in the faithful observance of the austere Carmelite rule of prayer, self-abasement, and penance. During those years, moreover, her soul has become marvellously strengthened and perfected in the life-giving climate of *Spiritual Childhood*, in the *Little Way* which Thérèse, during her last three years on earth, traced out for the sister who was also her novice.

Having run as a giant the full length of that Way, this former novice in this *Memoir* gives us now a look at the foundation on which this life of simplicity and littleness was built. As the road of *Spiritual Childhood* is not obstructed by many books of rules and regulations—its only set formula calling for a certain habitual disposition of heart—Soeur Geneviève has chosen the very best means of transcribing for us the content of the Saint's teaching. She merely repeats with authentic detail Thérèse's counsels to her novices and reconstructs their conversations together.

Before her death, Thérèse of Lisieux wrote that even were she to live until the age of eighty she would continue to run in her *Little Way of Spiritual Childhood*. Her sister Céline, now in her eighty-ninth year, has done just that. In doing so she has not only added a deathless dimension to the *Little Way of Spiritual Childhood*, but she has become once again for Thérèse, and in startling fashion, " the sweet echo of my soul."

THE CARMELITES OF NEW YORK.

LETTERS OF APPROBATION

LETTER FROM HIS EXCELLENCY MOST REVEREND RAYMOND A. LANE, M.M., D.D., FORMER SUPERIOR GENERAL OF MARYKNOLL FOREIGN MISSION SOCIETY OF AMERICA.

Dear Reverend Mother:

Your request for a letter of introduction to the English translation of Soeur Geneviève's *Memoir* of Saint Thérèse, has revived in my mind the memory of my first meeting with the Little Flower.

In the year 1924, there occurred a very serious strike in Hong Kong. Anti-foreign feeling was strong throughout China and especially in the South. In the city of Hong Kong itself, almost to a man, the Chinese refused to work, and essential services were in a perilous state. Naturally, the non-Chinese had to step into the breach: government officials milked cows at the dairy farms; British soldiers manned the ferry boats; Christian Brothers handled the mail. Everyone volunteered for something.

To complete an already serious situation, rumours were started that terrified the Chinese and the foreigners as well: the government was going to poison the water supply, and the Chinese, at a given signal, were to rise up and kill all the foreigners. Ship after ship left Hong Kong for Canton so heavily loaded with humanity that the vessels were soon deep in water, far above the safety line.

The Bishop of Hong Kong, worried like everyone else, decided on a Triduum to the Little Flower. I was asked to preach it. I must admit right here that I was one of those who had made light of this new devotion without having investigated it—a common error indeed. And so, I "backed into" the devotion, as it were, forced by duty.

One of our priests, a friend of Thérèse from the beginning, had given me the large edition of the French life, *Histoire d'une Ame*, along with many other "things to be read when there is time." We were living at that time in a section of Hong Kong known as West Point, and in our house the book had its place on a shelf. It would have gone on gathering dust there had I not been suddenly faced with this Triduum, and the need to acquire all information available about Thérèse of Lisieux.

I had felt that devotion to the Little Flower was emotional and superficial. But now, as I read on, I discovered that only hardy souls could imitate her. I had thought that there was too much propaganda about her, but I now became convinced there was not enough. I had not known of her "missionary vocation"—at least not clearly—and I now found her to be an old friend of my old friend, Theophane Venard.

In other words, from a cold, uninterested observer, I had become an enthusiastic follower. Has not this indeed been the experience of many?

Our little Saint has, moreover, stood the test of time; her charm perdures. True, other saints have taken the stage—Mother Cabrini, Martin de Porres, Maria Goretti, Pius X. But the Little Flower remains the great favourite.

All the friends and clients of Saint Thérèse will give a warm welcome to the English version of this *Memoir*. May it help to bring to them three things sorely needed in our day: an appreciation of suffering as necessary for the glory of God and the salvation of souls; a deep confidence in the mercy of God; a sense of urgency about the conversion of mankind.

Few have had a clearer vision than Saint Thérèse of what true devotion to the Mother of God means, based on the solid and unexaggerated motive of Mary's life, and her part in our Redemption. Our congratulations, therefore, to the Carmelite Nuns of New York City for this English translation which they completed during the Marian year.

✠ RAYMOND A. LANE, M.M., D.D.,
Maryknoll Generalate,
Maryknoll, N.Y.

LETTER OF
HIS EXCELLENCY MONSIGNOR SALVATORE NATUCCI

Sacred Congregation of Rites,
January 30, 1952.

Dear Reverend Mother Prioress: [1]

I am returning herewith the manuscript of the *Memoir* which has been dictated by the heart rather than by the pen of our dear " Céline." [2]

These reminiscences become a valuable and precious complement to the autobiographical writings of her immortal sister, Thérèse of Lisieux, a Saint who is little and great at one and the same time.

More than forty years ago when His Holiness, Pius X [3] was writing to thank your Carmel for his copy of Soeur Thérèse's *Autobiography*, he bore witness to the young Carmelite in the following words:

" This volume, wherein the virtues of the Virgin of Lisieux shine forth with such splendour, and into which she seems to have poured out her very soul, has filled us with an indefinable joy. Truly, she has flowered as a lily, she has shed abroad a sweet odour, she has brought forth a

---

[1] Mère Françoise-Thérèse, Prioress of the Carmel of Lisieux.

[2] Last surviving sister of Saint Thérèse—Soeur Geneviève.

[3] Now Saint Pius X.

true efflorescence of divine graces. She has praised with canticles and has blessed the Lord in all His works."

These sentiments of the saintly pontiff sum up my own reaction to this new publication. Moreover, a deep abiding joy takes possession of me when I realize that from its perennial source at the Carmel of Lisieux this pure fragrance is still reaching legions of souls and drawing them safely along Saint Thérèse's *Little Way*.

With prayerful good wishes to you, Very Reverend Mother, to our very dear " Céline, and to all at Carmel, I am,

Very Devotedly Yours,
SALVATORE NATUCCI,
Promoter General of the Faith.

INTRODUCTION

In the large edition of Saint Thérèse's *Autobiography*, the supplementary chapter entitled *Counsels and Reminiscences* was taken from the depositions which her former novices had prepared for the Canonical Process of the Beatification and Canonization. The present work, however, consists only of those counsels received by Soeur Geneviève de la Sainte Face, the Saint's sister, Céline, who, as we all know, held a privileged place in Thérèse's affections.

Céline was not only her sister according to the flesh but also her disciple in the spiritual order. Thérèse was referring to this when she wrote in her *Autobiography*, " I can truly say that my affection for her (Céline) was rather that of a mother than of a sister, and I was filled with solicitude for the welfare of her soul." The Saint returns to the subject when on July 16, 1897, in one of her last conversations with Reverend Mère Agnès de Jésus, she said, " I had made a complete sacrifice of Céline's presence, but I cannot say I no longer desired to have her enter here. Often in the summer during the hour of Great Silence before Matins when I was on the terrace, I used to think to myself, ' Oh, if only my Céline were here, right beside me . . . but then that would be too great happiness ' . . .

And it seemed an impossible dream. It was not, however, in view of any natural satisfaction that I desired this happiness. It was rather in the interests of Céline's soul and that she might follow our *Little Way*. And when later I saw her not only enter here but given over entirely to me for instruction, it was then that I realized how God infinitely surpassed my desires, and I understood how tremendously He loved me . . ."

These observations accentuate the importance of the reminiscences which follow. Their great historical value stems from the fact that they are extracts from the following sources:

1. The personal notes which Soeur Geneviève, in obedience to Mère Agnès de Jésus, had already recorded while Saint Thérèse was alive. The Saint was aware of the existence of these rough drafts and gave them her unqualified approval.

2. From Soeur Geneviève's depositions prepared for the Canonical Process. These pages contain in substance all these depositions.

Recently, Soeur Geneviève de la Sainte Face added some new reminiscences to this *Memoir*.

The divisions of the work and their titles have been made in view of publication.

A short time after the death of Thérèse, when Soeur Geneviève was gathering together these personal souvenirs in a notebook, she wrote the following introduction:

J.M.J.T.

" In my childhood I often read the lives of the saints, and these stories used to inspire me and inflame my heart. They intensified my yearning after the good and the beautiful, and they guided and enraptured the years of my youth . . . By this means, I caught a glimpse of the ideal of sanctity, and how often I used to day-dream about it ! Yet I had never made any living contact with it, for in order to touch something, we must be very close to it. And if our admiration for the saints be genuine, we must be ready to imitate these heroes who have inspired it. At Carmel, however, I found in our dear little Soeur Thérèse all that I had been searching for and, through her, all these desires were realized.

" O Mary, my Mother ! It is beneath your gentle gaze that I commit to writing these reminiscences. In the day of trial and temptation, in the hour of darkness, may I remember that these things were said to me by the Angel whom you sent to guide my first steps in the religious life. And now, from the height of Heaven, she will, I know, continue to accompany and guide me to the very last hour of my life."

Soeur Geneviève, now (November 1957) in her eighty-ninth year, has recently examined these notes which she wrote at the beginning of her religious life at the dictation, as it were, of her saintly little sister. Her task finished, she concludes her *Memoir* with the following moving testimony.

> " I have re-read and classified these reminiscences which were recorded in personal notebooks, and in my deposition for the Double Process. Most of these memoirs are conversational in form and thus we have the contrast of ' the voice of nature and the voice of grace ' of the Imitation. In some places, although the ' voice of nature ' becomes repetitious even to the point of being wearisome, I have thought it best to suppress nothing so that no slight accent of the ' voice of grace ' might be missed.
>
> " May these souvenirs assist many other souls in their efforts to overcome their faults and imperfections.
>
> " I hereby affirm that these pages are in all truth conformable to all that I saw and heard.— *Soeur Geneviève de la Sainte Face et de Sainte Thérèse, O.C.D., June 9, 1951.*"

This document speaks for itself, and gives better than we could ever hope to give the reason for this publication. It was Soeur Geneviève who depicted on canvas the Agonizing Face of her Divine Master as It was mysteriously revealed on the Winding Sheet of Turin. It was she who consecrated her artistic talent to the faithful reproduction of a physical portrait of her saintly sister. And now, with scrupulous fidelity, it is she who recounts these anecdotes and sayings which definitively trace out for us the moral portrait of Saint Thérèse of the Child Jesus. No other work could more effectively excite our admiration and our desire for imitation.

THE CARMELITES OF LISIEUX

MY SISTER
ST. THÉRÈSE

CHAPTER I

THE MISTRESS OF NOVICES

WHEN, on February 20, 1893, my sister, Mère Agnès de Jésus, became Prioress of the Carmel of Lisieux, she confided to her predecessor, Mère Marie de Gonzague, the office of Novice Mistress. A few days later, Mère Agnès asked our youngest sister, Thérèse,[1] to interest herself in a tactful way with the spiritual life of her companions in the novitiate, to receive their confidences, and to guide them in the ways of the religious life. Two lay sisters, Marthe de Jésus, and Marie Madeline de la Sainte Sacrement, were the only novices other than Thérèse in the monastery at the time. Soeur Marie de la Trinité had already joined them (June 16, 1894) when I came to the novitiate on September 14th of the same year. The entrance of Marie Guérin, our cousin, in August of the next year,[2] brought the number of novices up to five.

When, in March 1896, Mère de Gonzague was elected Prioress again, she decided to combine this office with the functions of Novice Mistress.

---

[1] The Saint was then twenty years of age.

[2] August 15, 1895. Soeur Marie de l'Eucharistie.

On the advice of Mère Agnès, however, she soon enlisted the aid of our Saint who had acquitted herself of the office of assistant with such remarkable aptitude during the preceding three years. The full direction of the novitiate then fell to Thérèse who—without bearing the title—filled the office of Mistress until her death on September 30, 1897.

It was only after Mère de Gonzague's election in 1896 that Thérèse, in an official capacity assembled the novices together for daily instruction after Vespers (2.30 to 3 in the afternoon according to our custom at that time). Usually there was no formal conference, for hers was not a systematized spiritual education. The period of novitiate instruction began with the reading of a section of the *Rule*, the *Constitutions*, or the *Custom Book*.[3]   After some necessary explanation or comments Soeur Thérèse would answer the questions which we put to her; and if we had committed any faults, the correction would then take place. For the rest of the time she conversed with us on any subject of interest

---

[3] Discalced Carmelites observe the Primitive Rule of Carmel which was drawn up by Albert of Vercelli, Patriarch of Jesuralem, and promulgated in the year 1247.

It was on this Rule that Saint Teresa of Avila based her *Constitutions* which are still in force in all the Teresian Carmels in the world. The *Custom Book*, while not possessing the same binding force as the *Constitutions*, is followed as far as possible in all Carmelite Monasteries, with certain adaptations required by the customs and trends of various countries.

at the moment, and familiarized herself with all that concerned our spiritual life or even our domestic work about the monastery.

* * *

In her direction of the novices the Saint always adapted her counsel to the particular need of the soul in question. She enlightened our consciences, and solved our problems according to our individual temperaments, our personal needs, or our actual trials or joys. From her own words we learn that the wise Mistress was keenly aware that a spiritual counsel profitable to one soul might be meaningless—or even harmful—to another. The following passage from her *Autobiography* bears witness to the rare gift of spiritual discernment which was ever manifest in her training of the novices. She writes:

" . . . I realized that, while for the most part all souls have the same battles, yet no two souls are exactly alike. It was easy then for me to understand what Father Pichon used to say: ' There are as many shades of differences among souls as there are in human countenances.' Each soul, therefore, should be dealt with in a different way . . . Our own tastes, our personal ideas must be forgotten, and we must guide souls

not by our own way but along that particular
path which Jesus indicates.[4]

" . . . What would happen if an ill-instructed
gardener did not properly graft his trees; if,
without understanding the nature of each, he
should try, for instance, to grow roses on a
peach tree? The tree, which had been vigorous
and, perhaps, gave promise of much fruit, would
simply wither away.

" How important it is to be able to recognize
God's claims on the individual soul, even from
early childhood, so that instead of anticipating
or hindering it we might, rather, second the
action of divine grace in the lives of others
 . . . "[5]

Saint Thérèse made these wise observations
about the spiritual education of children.   But
how well she knew how to apply the principle
when there was question of the guidance of souls,
the chief task of a novice-mistress !

In the study of this *Memoir*, therefore, let
us make a similar distinction, and each reader
may take to himself that advice or counsel which
is best adapted to his individual needs.

Although our holy Mistress was remarkably
sweet in character, she was also very firm.   She
never overlooked anything in the novices which
needed correction.   As soon as she noticed

---

[4] Original manuscript of St. Thérèse's *Autobiography*, Ms C.,
fol. 23v, 22v.

[3] *Ibid.* Ms. A., fol. 53r.

something at fault, she would hurry to find the
" culprit " to take her to task. This was not at
all easy for her to do; nevertheless, she let
nothing prevent her from doing her duty.

She assures us that whenever truth was in the
balance she feared nothing and would in fact go
out to meet the enemy. She gave proof of this
one day shortly before her death when, burning
with fever and suffering from a tuberculous
throat which seemed to be on fire, she summoned up all her strength and vigour in order
to admonish a novice who was at fault. Later
she said to me, " You see, I must die with my
weapons in hand—and in my mouth ' the sword
of the Spirit which is the Word of God '." [6]

In one of our intimate conversations, Sister
Thérèse of the Child Jesus told me:

> " Ever since I took over the novitiate, my life has
> been one of war and struggle . . . But the good
> God has done the work for me. I have laboured
> for Him and my soul has made astounding
> progress . . . My only desire has been to please
> Him; consequently I have not worried over
> what others might be thinking or saying about
> me. I have not sought to be loved for myself,
> nor have I desired that my efforts bear fruit.
> True, we must sow the seed of goodness on all
> sides, but if it does not spring up, what matter !

[6] Eph. VI, 17, and the Rule of Carmel.

Our lot is to work; the victory is for Jesus.
When there is question of doing good to our
neighbour, we must let nothing deter us nor pass
over anything to make things easier for ourselves.
As for reprimands, our intention in giving them
must be directed first to the glory of God and
must not spring from a desire to succeed in
enlightening the novices. Moreover, in order
that a correction bear fruit, it must *cost* in the
giving, and the heart must be free from the least
shadow of passion."

This testimony interprets the Saint's complete
thought on the subject. I often had cause to
marvel at her wonderful spirit of renunciation
in her contacts with the novices, how patiently
she listened to us and instructed us without ever
seeming to desire any joy or distraction for self.
No less remarkable was her disinterested zeal
in the case of those novices who were less
favourably endowed; towards them she always
manifested the greatest affection. It was evident
that she was never influenced by external
appearances but always maintained a universal
reverence and respect for the soul for its own
sake.

Soeur Thérèse was in the habit of quoting
to us texts from Holy Scripture in order to
emphasize a particular lesson, and when replying
to our questions she usually illustrated the point
by a story. In this way, she succeeded in

impressing on our memories the truths which she desired to instil into our souls.

I was often lost in admiration on seeing how clearly she detected the wiles of nature, and how well she succeeded in regulating the diverse movements of our souls. She seemed to possess a supernatural discernment, and this to such a degree that we were sometimes led to believe that she could actually read our souls. We were convinced that she was truly inspired from on high, and whenever I consulted her it was with the firm belief that the Holy Spirit of God would answer me through her. But there was not any extraordinary external manifestation in all this, for she was simplicity itself; she never suspected that any powerful grace might be going out from her.

* * *

The novices inconvenienced her in season and out of season, but she was uniformly calm and full of sweetness on all occasions. They often interrupted her work and plagued her with indiscreet questions, especially when she was writing her autobiography or engaged on a letter to one of her spiritual brothers. Not once did I ever hear her answer them impatiently, nor even abruptly or hastily.

HER PRUDENCE

At the beginning of her life as Novice-Mistress, our dear little Sister used to strive to put an end to our interior conflicts either by reasoning with us or by trying to convince us in our little difficulties in the novitiate that our companions were not at fault. She soon realized that this method only served to open up long useless discussions, with no profit whatsoever to our souls, so she adopted another means. Instead of trying to close the issue by denying that there was any cause for complaint, she would urge us rather to face reality. Let me illustrate the point by an example.

If one of the novices had failed in her appointed duty and had, as a result, inconvenienced the rest of us in the novitiate, I might go to Thérèse at the end of the week with a complaint like this: " Here it is Saturday and, evidently, Sister X has not given a thought to her weekly assignment. This annoys me for you know how conscientious I am whenever this duty falls to me in the novitiate ! "

Thérèse would then seem to become interested. Without minimizing the tantalizing side of the situation (and apparently with no desire to make me ashamed of myself for complaining) she would invite me to examine the details at closer range. " Suppose," the Saint would say, " that your companion is as blameworthy as you believe her to be . . . " and so on. This was her way of proving to me that she was ready to listen and not over-eager to rebuke me immediately. Such an attitude, as she had anticipated, would have its pacifying effect on me, and from there on it was easy for her to lead me step by step to a more virtuous disposition of soul.

It would not be long until I should find myself rejoicing that I had been imposed on, and would even begin to desire that all the Sisters should utterly disregard me and show me no consideration at any time.

Neither would the promptings of divine grace cease at that point, for I would soon feel springing up within me very generous *desires* to be scolded and to bear alone the blame whenever my companions neglected any duty—or even to be reproached for some careless piece of work in which I had had no part whatsoever.

It was by such methods that Thérèse would have me soon established in an attitude of mind that was close to perfection. The victory assured, she would proceed to relate in detail the countless acts of hidden virtue which the novice in question had often practised. A warm admiration would then replace my critical thoughts and I was ready to believe that all the Sisters were far more virtuous than I.

If it happened that even while I was complaining, Thérèse knew that the tardy novice had finally accomplished the appointed task, and though she was also aware that this knowledge should have put an end to my uncharitable temptation at the outset, the Saint, nevertheless, would withhold the information from me until the propitious moment.

At other times, she might wait for us to make these discoveries for ourselves; then we needed no further proof that often the negligences and faults which we impute to others are no more than the figments of our imaginations.

That there should be interior struggles over such trifles in the religious life might come as a surprise to many readers. I confess that at the beginning of my Carmelite life I also experienced some astonishment at this very thing. To me it seemed that, having made the supreme sacrifice of complete separation from loved ones, and utter renunciation of the world, it should have been relatively easy to bear the thousand and one minor crosses of community life. My own petty re-actions, however, to the personal trials that came my way shortly after my entrance disabused me of this false notion.

It is well to remember that with those living in the world, such trifles very frequently provoke similar re-actions. But the innumerable distractions of the active life necessarily divert the attention from such vexations, at least for a time, and thus the edge is taken off the annoyance.

The cloister, on the other hand, is foreign to all such distraction, and it is possible that self-love under such circumstances is more alert to the little misunderstandings which arise. We should also bear in mind that the life of the cloister calls for the frequent contact and close relationship of the most diverse characters and temperaments—of persons whose assimilation of spiritual principles is often conditioned by their early education and home environment.

Experience has proved that it is quite possible for a religious in the cloister to bear up heroically under the greatest tortures of body and soul, and on the other hand, to experience a death-like struggle in the face of trifling disturbances. But this striving for self-mastery inasmuch as it is unceasing and sustained, is particularly meritorious; hence the frequent avowal of an old experienced religious: " My chalice? It is community life ! "

The struggle is, moreover, the price of that exquisite charity which flourishes in our monasteries. Saint Thérèse, who had learned to soar high above such trials and maintain her soul in peace, was ever on the alert to show us how to surmount these hurdles in community life. It was in these " little struggles " over annoyances and natural repugnances or re-actions to trifling, almost picayune, vexations that the virtues of her *Little Way* and the practice of the doctrine of " Littleness " always triumphed.

As I was her sister and her novice, Thérèse conversed with me freely about my interior life, since she was directing me. Nevertheless, there were many occasions when I saw her deliberately overcoming a desire to pour out her heart to me. She spoke of none of her own trials to us in the novitiate, for she believed, on principle, that a superior must forget herself entirely.

In this connection she pointed out a certain temptation which sometimes comes to those in charge when subjects confide to them their physical sufferings or other acute personal trials. Almost unconsciously at such times some superiors have a tendency to complain of the same or similar afflictions. It was different with Soeur Thérèse. She helped us in every way but did so without a shade of self-interest and with no thought of deriving any consolation for her own heart.

She told me confidentially that when she became our Mistress, she had begged God, above all, not to allow the novices to love her with any mere human affection. It was evident that her prayer had been granted, for although the novices all loved her to an extraordinary degree, there was never anything childish or sentimental in our relations with her. We used to have recourse to her simply to satisfy our thirst for truth and not, as is often the temptation with young religious, merely to enjoy the company of the Mistress.[7]

Even some other nuns of the community, grown old in the practices of the Carmelite life, and recognizing the Saint's rare gift of supernatural prudence, used to come privately to consult her. Her unusual spiritual influence over souls stemmed from her virtuous life, and was the reward of her life of prayer and total abnegation, which were her chief means of winning souls to God. She frequently raised her heart to God during her conferences with us, and I often became aware of this interior movement of her soul.

* * *

HER HUMILITY

Although there was a constant interplay of all the virtues in the life of Soeur Thérèse, it was the virtue of humility, beyond all question, which attained its greatest triumph in her soul. It was in order to become more humble and to descend to a still lower level of " littleness," that

---

[7] " Sister Thérèse of the Child Jesus never sought to curry favour with the novices by any trick of human prudence, and this was one of the remarkable features of her direction of the novitiate. Her only desire was to assist the young religious in their struggle for perfection, and for this end she neglected no means in her power, even if it were a question of losing their affection. I could give numerous instances which emphasize this fidelity to conscience in her relations with the novices."—Deposition of Mère Agnès de Jésus at the Process of Canonization-Summarium 1552.

she set out on the *Way of Spiritual Childhood*;
and it was because of her fidelity in following
this *Way* that she became as humble and simple
as a little child.

* * *

Thérèse always experienced a particular joy
in remembering that in spite of having spent
almost ten years in the religious life, she had
never left the novitiate. Consequently, she was
classed among the " little ones " of the community inasmuch as she was not a member of
the conventual chapter.[8]

It was when we were all crushed to the earth
by the humiliating trial of our beloved father's
illness that Thérèse gave evident proofs that her
desire for contempt was genuine and deeply
rooted in her soul.

Ever since her early years, she had loved to
repeat with holy enthusiasm this prayer of Saint
John of the Cross: " Lord to suffer and to be

---

[8] Normally, Soeur Thérèse should have left the novitiate in
September 1893, three years after profession and become a
member of the community chapter immediately, if a current
interpretation of the law had not automatically excluded her.
Not more than two members of a family, according to this ordin-
ance, could participate in a community chapter and as the two
older Martins, Soeur Agnès de Jésus and Soeur Marie du Sacré-
Coeur, had already been accepted, their younger sister, Thérèse,
had to step aside. It is true that she was charged with the direction
of the novitiate but only under the control of the official Mistress;
actually she was simply the " senior " of the novitiate all her life.

despised for Thee." This was the theme of all our aspirations during those memorable evenings of our last summer together at home.

* * *

In her *Autobiography* the Saint gives us a graphic description of these summer evenings of 1887 at Les Buissonets.[9] She writes:

> " Céline had become the intimate sharer of my thoughts and aspirations. Since the grace of the preceding Christmas, we understood each other perfectly. The difference in age [10] no longer mattered as I had grown to be a tall young girl and, more important still, I had also advanced in grace . . . Desiring that we go forward together along the path of virtue, Jesus united us by ties stronger than blood; we had become sisters in spirit.
>
> > ' In the track of Thy footprint
> > The young girls run along the way.
> > At the touch of a spark, at the spiced wine,
> > Flows forth the divine balsam.'

[9] (In Soeur Geneviève's *Conseils et Souvenirs* this commentary on the conversations of those summer evenings at Les Buissonets is given only as an Appendix. For practical purposes, however, we have placed it here. This relation of the graces of that period had been written by Soeur Geneviève, some time ago, to comply with the urgent request of an eminent Jesuit who desired a detailed account. Consequently, it does not form an integral part of these *Memoirs*).

[10] Céline was almost four years older than Thérèse.

"This verse of the *Spiritual Canticle* [11] of Our Father, Saint John of the Cross, was truly verified in us at this period of our lives. It was indeed with light heart that we followed in the footprints of Jesus. The sparks of love which He so bountifully enkindled in our souls and the strong, delicious wine which He gave us to drink made us utterly oblivious to all created things. We no longer knew any other language than those aspirations of love which He had inspired in our hearts.

"What tender memories are revived as I recall our conversations each evening together at Les Buissonets. As we gazed out into the vast expanse, we could watch the pale moon leisurely coming out behind the tall trees . . . enveloping drowsy nature in its silver light, while the deep azure vault scintillated with brilliant stars . . . and the soft breath of evening seemed to be scattering the snowy clouds. The view of the panorama raised our hearts to heaven, to that true heaven into which we were peering, and of which it served as a reflecting curtain.

"I may be mistaken, but it seems to me that the outpouring of our hearts resembled that of Saint Monica and her son Augustine when at the port of Ostia they remained lost in ecstasy at sight of the wonders of the Creator. I believe that the graces we received might well be compared to those granted to the great saints.

"'God,' says the *Imitation*, 'communicates

---

[11] Spiritual Canticle of Saint John of the Cross, Stanza xxv.

Himself sometimes amid dazzling light, and at other times, sweetly veiled under types and figures.' [12] It was in this latter way that He deigned to manifest Himself to our souls; but how *light* and *transparent* was the veil concealing Jesus from our eyes . . . Doubt was no longer possible; Faith and Hope had already given place to Love, Love which enabled us to find even on earth Him whom we were seeking. And when He found us alone ' He gave us His kiss that no one might henceforth despise us.' [13]

"Such overwhelming graces could not but bear abundant fruit, and the practice of virtue gradually became sweet and natural to me. In the beginning my looks would often betray the struggle, but little by little this too was overcome, and then self-sacrifice, even at the first prompting, became easy . . ." [14]

This description which Thérèse has given in her *Autobiography*, far from being exaggerated, seems to me to fall short of the actual reality. As though they took place yesterday, I can recall these conversations at Les Buissonets; so deep is the impression they have left on my soul. Those were indeed hours of heavenly consolation for both of us, consolations which could hardly be described in words . . .

---

[12] Cf. Imit., Book III, Chapter 43.

[13] Cf. Cant. VIII—1.

[14] Original manuscript of St. Therese's *Autobiography*, Ms. A., fol. 47v, 48r.

With our hearts lifted up to heaven, we would repeat to each other Abbé Arminjon's inspiring words: " And God in His gratitude shall exclaim ' Now it is my turn '." As our Saint has written: " Faith and Hope had already given place to Love." In spirit we were no longer on earth; it was in truth the possession of God in Love.

After all these years I can definitely say that the graces we received were not mere accidental flashes of light nor were they the result of some transient outbursts of fervour.   No, on the contrary, they produced in our souls a steady and consistent reaching out towards God; we seemed to belong no longer to this earth. Indeed it could be called *ecstasy*.

I have been asked to define in precise terms the meaning of the word ecstasy as I use it here, and I should like to explain that this ecstasy did not deprive us of consciousness nor raise us from the ground. I can still see Thérèse, her beautiful eyes bathed in tears, pressing my hand in hers; as she herself has written, our communings resembled those of Saint Monica and Saint Augustine at the port of Ostia.

* * *

" That which we need more than anything else," the Saint used to tell me, " is humility of heart, and you cannot believe you possess it until you are willing to let everybody order you about. You are pleasant enough so long as you can have your own way about things, but as soon as your opinion is ignored or contradicted you become dejected. Is there any virtue in all that? No, for real virtue ' is to be submissive under the hand of all,' [15] which means to be happy whenever you are blamed for anything whatsoever. At the beginning this will not be easy, and your countenance will probably betray the effort. Then others will judge you to be imperfect still. That is the best feature of the whole matter because you will then be practising humility—which really consists not only in thinking and in saying that you are full of imperfections but in being glad that others also think that you are imperfect—and even say so.

" You know," she said, " we should be very happy that our neighbour sometimes criticizes and condemns us, for if no one were engaged in this business, what would become of us? It is our opportunity for making a little profit . . . "

* * *

Soeur Thérèse had provided a spiritual entertainment for one of our community feasts, and because it proved to be too long, she was found fault with and the little performance was broken

[15] Imit., Bk. III, Chap. XLIV, 7.

off. A few moments later, I happened to come upon her in one of the alcoves and found her quietly drying a few tears. She had herself soon under control, however, and remained peaceful and sweet in spite of the humiliation.[16]

It was really with supernatural happiness that she accepted all reproaches not only from Superiors but even inferiors. She always allowed the novices to criticize her freely and if she was bound to correct them for any of their disparaging remarks about her, she never did so at the moment of the humiliation.

* * *

I told Soeur Thérèse one day that if I must be reproached I preferred deserving it to being unjustly accused. " For my part," she answered, " it is quite the contrary. I *prefer* to be rebuked unjustly because, in that case, having nothing to reproach myself with, I gladly offer the little injustice to God. Then I go a step further and humble myself in thinking how easily I might have committed the fault of which I had been accused."

---

[16] The entertainment in question was a playlet entitled *The Flight into Egypt*, which Thérèse had composed for the Feast of Saint Agnes, January 21, 1896. It was the *Hymn of the Angel in the Desert* which caused the interruption.

" To me humility is truth," Thérèse said to me quite simply one day. " I do not know whether I am humble, but I do know that I see the truth in all things."

In her private interviews with the novices, she was always returning to the virtue of humility. The foundation of her teaching on this subject was that we should not lose heart at the sight of our weakness but rather *glory* in in our infirmities. " It is so sweet to *feel* our weakness and littleness," she often told us.

She always placed herself in the class of the weak and imperfect, and wanted us to do the same. It was in this way that we began to use the expression " little souls." [17]

---

[17] In his Christmas message, December 23, 1949, His Holiness, Pope Pius XII, deplored the error of those who would have us believe that " sin is a simple weakness of human nature " and who even " mistake this weakness for virtue." All Saint Thérèse's teaching on confidence and abandonment finds its echo in these sentiments of the Sovereign Pontiff, for we know how vigorously she denounced the specious error of quietism. It is abundantly clear, moreover, that the Saint never advocated a passive acceptance of our faults, however slight they might be. To her, such an attitude would have seemed to be derogatory to the law of God.

On the contrary, she continually emphasizes, through her *Little Doctrine*, our fundamental need as creatures to trust neither in our own power nor in our merits. We should, rather, lean entirely on divine grace which alone has the power to inspire, to assist, and to strengthen our wills and to crown all our efforts in this life.

We are not excusing or making light of our sin by the mere fact that we recognize or even love our weakness and accept all its consequences. No, in this way, as a matter of fact, we become established in truth and we are saved from all self-delusion. Then from the very depths of our misery, which we then recognize better than ever before, there springs up a cry of daring confidence

On a certain occasion when Soeur Thérèse had pointed out my many faults to me, I became rather sad and felt quite helpless.

" Here I am," I lamented, " farther away than ever from my goal. It seems that the more I desire to advance in virtue, the worse I become. I long to become sweet and patient, humble and charitable, but I do not think I shall ever succeed . . . "

At prayer that evening, I read that on one occasion when Saint Gertrude had expressed the same sentiments, Our Lord answered her: " In

---

in the infinite mercy of God. That pays in full for all our weaknesses, for all our fits of depression, and all our temptations, for all the trials, imperfections, and falls to which our frail human nature is heir. It throws light on the matter to learn that the novices to whom Saint Thérèse used to address these counsels were particularly inclined to a spirit of discouragement because of such human frailties.

The closing paragraphs of Chapter X of the *Autobiography*, with their moving commentary on the mercy of God, and other Thérèsian texts, prove beyond question that with slight modifications this doctrine concerning our attitude towards our falls and weakness applies even to our sins and back-slidings of the past. It makes no difference if our sins be as crushing as those of the Samaritan woman or the woman taken in adultery, of the good thief on the cross, or of the penitent sinner in the desert. Once again, we do not love our sins; no, we bitterly repent of them and strive with all our will to prevent their recurrence. But, far from despairing over them or from giving in to a proud and disagreeable impatience because of them, we use them rather to deepen our distrust of self. We then go on to a greater confidence in God's merciful love which forgives completely, raises us up at once, and overwhelms us with His favours and with His love. That makes up for everything. Thérèse quotes in this connection the celebrated maxim of Saint Augustine who, interpreting and completing Saint Paul's thought, writes: " For those who love God, all things —even sin—work together unto good."

all things and above all things, hold on to your *good will*, for this disposition alone will impart to your soul the splendour and the special merit of all the virtues. He who possesses this good will, this sincere desire to advance My Glory, to thank Me and to compassionate My Sufferings, to love and to serve Me as much as all creatures combined, will, without any doubt, receive a reward compatible with My Infinite Goodness. Furthermore, it might sometimes happen that one soul would derive more profit from such a desire than some other soul might gain from the performance of good works."

These words of Our Lord made me very happy, for they brought me the encouragement I needed. I hastened to repeat them to my dear little Mistress who commented on them and added:

> " Do you know that the *Life of Father Surin* [18] contains a striking passage on this subject of good will? He had just performed an exorcism and the demons confessed; ' We are victorious on all sides, yet, when it comes to this little watch-dog whose name is *good will*, we must always yield.' And so," Thérèse continued, " even if you are without virtue, you at least have ' a little watch-dog ' who will save you from all danger. Be consoled, for it will eventually bring you to heaven !—Ah ! Where is the soul who does not desire with all her

---

[18] *Vie du Père Joseph Surin, S.J.*, par le Père Marcel Bouix, Paris 1879; p. 146.

heart to possess the virtues? This longing is common to us all. On the other hand, how very few there are in the spiritual life who are willing to fail, to stumble and fall, to be happy when others find them prostrate on the ground!"

* * *

One day when I was ascribing my state of discouragement and depression to physical fatigue, the Saint said to me:

"Whenever you are lacking in virtue, you should not excuse yourself by throwing the blame on physical causes, on the weather, or some other trial. Instead, you should make it a means of self-humiliation, and then go to take your place in the rank and file of *little souls*, since you are so weak in the practice of virtue. Your soul's urgent need at present is not the ability to practise heroic virtue, but rather to acquire humility. For this end, your acts of self-conquest themselves must have some admixture of imperfection so that you will not be able to dwell on them with any degree of self-complacency. Rather just to recall them will humble and remind you that you are not holy. There are some souls who, as long as they live, will find that they are never appreciated. This makes it impossible for them ever to think they possess those virtues which they admire in others."

Soeur Thérèse one day confided to me, "Recently, in the presence of one of the nuns I acted in a very natural way but, as the struggle was only interior, I was convinced that Sister had not noticed the imperfection. But do you know what I did? I purposely entertained the thought that Sister had noticed my lack of virtue, and I cannot tell you how happy I was while humbling myself in this way."

On a similar occasion she told me, "It fills me with joy to have been imperfect;[19] today God has granted me great graces; it has been a profitable day indeed . . ."

When I asked how anyone could entertain such noble sentiments, she answered, "My little method consists in this—rejoicing always and continually smiling—in times of defeat as well as victory."

Thérèse, with her strong virtuous soul, was, however, so distrustful of self that she easily believed herself capable of committing the greatest sins. Underneath a picture of Jesus on the Cross, she wrote these words: "O Lord, Thou knowest well that I love Thee[20] . . . but have pity on me for I am a sinner."[21] These

---

[19] "In spite of my sincere efforts to have acted in a virtuous manner," Soeur Thérèse would have added had she been asked to explain. This honest effort, as pointed out previously, must always be presupposed when Soeur Thérèse makes statements of this nature.

[20] John, XXI-15.   [21] Luke, XVIII-3.

sentiments indicate the habitual dispositions of her soul.

*   *   *

The Saint told me of an incident which enabled her to lay the finger on her human frailty and fickleness—a fault from which none of us can hope to be entirely free as long as we live.

She had been hoping against hope to enter Carmel on the first anniversary of her " conversion " of Christmas 1886. The extraordinary means she had taken having utterly failed, she was in consequence disconsolate to find herself still in the outside world on Christmas Day of 1887.

" And yet," the Saint added when relating this story to me, " would you believe that, in spite of the ocean of bitterness inundating my soul, I experienced a real pleasure on that Christmas night in wearing my pretty blue hat with the white dove.[22]   What tricks this human nature of ours can play on us ! "

*   *   *

I told her that I noticed how even the persistence of a joy can become wearisome to us

[22] It was a small, brimless, navy-blue hat made from the same light-wool material as her dress and trimmed in matching velvet.

in this life. At times, I added, a happy thought
or even a holy sentiment, when we become
attached to it, ends only in fatigue. Thérèse
answered:

> " God alone is our rest, and the only joy which
> lasts is rooted solely in contempt of self . . .
> By the way about that affair last night . . . [23]
> Suppose Sister X thought that you were lacking
> in virtue; if deep in your heart, you agreed with
> her, that would indeed be a cause for true
> abiding joy."

" You are right," I replied. " The worst of it
is, I know what God expects of me, it is all very
clear, and yet I am able to do nothing about it.
I am convinced that I will never be any good."

" Yes, oh yes you will," Thérèse answered,
" for God Himself will see to that."

" Maybe so," I said, " but the nuns will never
be convinced. If I commit faults habitually, it is
only to be expected that I shall be considered
imperfect. It is not the same in your case, for
your virtue is recognized by all."

" Perhaps," she went on, " that is because I
have never desired to be considered perfect.
It is by far the better thing for you, however,
to be considered imperfect. There is your
chance for merit. Besides, true happiness can

---

[23] The evening before I had been exceptionally tired when on
duty in the Infirmary after Matins, and had shed a few tears in the
presence of one of the Sisters.

only be found in believing that others are virtuous and that we are the imperfect ones. Those who judge you unfavourably are not robbing you of anything; you are none the poorer for all they may say. It is they who are really the losers. And tell me, is there anything sweeter than the inward joy that comes from thinking well of others! If, for the love of God, you truly humble yourself when judged unfavourably by others, it is all the better for you and all the worse for your critics."

* * *

I confessed to her one day that I was in such a state as to be unable even to think. "That makes no difference," she told me. "God knows your intentions." Then to make me laugh, she used a little jargon familiar to us both and added, " *The humbler you are the happier you shall be*."

" Oh ! " I sighed. " When I think how much I have *to acquire* ! "

" Rather," she rejoined, " how much you have *to lose* ! . . . Jesus Himself will fill your soul with treasures in the same measure that you move your imperfections out of the way."

Thérèse often told me, " You will never reach perfection if you insist on *climbing* a mountain. What God wants of you is to *go down* to the heart of the fertile valley where you will learn to despise yourself."

I had taken this counsel of Saint Paul too literally: " Be careful to do good not only before God but also before men." [24]

I was intent on giving good example, and I desired to become a model of virtue for the other novices. Consequently, whenever I failed, I thought everything was lost.

" That is being self-centred," Thérèse told me, " and you mistake it for true zeal. What an illusion ! Listen to this story. Onec upon a time, a certain bishop and his attendants went to visit a Saint with a great reputation for holiness. At the bishop's approach, the holy man was, for a moment, tempted to vanity at the sight of a great prelate coming out with his suite to meet him. Desiring, however, at once, to humble himself for this fault, he quickly exchanged places with some children who were on a see-saw on the trunk of a tree nearby. The bishop, finding the saint at such a childish pastime, judged him rather to be an idiot and turned back without further inquiry. " You see," Thérèse added, " sometimes a soul who is not strong enough for praise must sacrifice for his own sanctification even a good which he might otherwise lawfully enjoy. So, you should be happy when you stumble and fall on the way to perfection. I would go even further and say that if in your fault there were no offence against

[24] Romans, XII—17.

God, you should really stumble on purpose in order to humble yourself."

* * *

Soeur Thérèse was never troubled by what others might be thinking about her, even when there was question of apparent disedification. For example, at the beginning of her illness, when she was obliged to take some medications a few minutes before meals,[25] an older Sister was surprised and began to blame the Saint for a want of regularity. Just one word of explanation from Thérèse would have been sufficient to exonerate herself and set the Sister's mind at ease. That explanation, however, the Saint would not give. Her model in this was Our Lady who preferred to lose her good name rather than reveal her secret to Saint Joseph. This simple yet heroic conduct of Our Lady was always an inspiration to Thérèse who often conversed with me about it. Like Mary, silence was her great weapon also, and she, too, loved to " keep all things in her heart," her joys as well as her sorrows. This reserve was her strength and the characteristic stamp of her perfection, even exteriorly, for her great poise and sense of proportion were evident in all her actions.

---

[25] In order to do this, she was obliged to leave a community exercise.

CHAPTER II

POVERTY OF SPIRIT

A S a remembrance of my profession my dear little sister made a sketch of my coat-of-arms with the motto I had chosen: " The loser always wins." [1] Later she developed this theme and went on to explain how we must choose to lose everything on this earth, and allow ourselves to be stripped of all, in order to gain poverty of spirit. In her own case she lived out this principle to such a degree as even to desire that others in preference to herself should be favoured by special graces. Moreover, I have seen her pass on to another a book from which she was deriving great spiritual profit, before she had finished reading it and without any hope of having it returned.

Whenever she received some spiritual illumination, she used to try to communicate it to others in so far as this was possible . . . At times, however, such interior impressions are so vivid and penetrating as to flash by without leaving behind any trace at all. Thérèse once told me: " Whenever I receive such lights and

---

[1] It was after this first attempt that she was inspired to sketch her own coat-of-arms.

then try to recapture them, it is usually impossible to do so. Instead of fatiguing my mind, therefore, by trying to probe the depths of my soul to discover the source of my joy, I simply taste in peace and happiness the heavenly sweetness that is flooding my soul. Oh, how happy I am in this practice of poverty of spirit . . . "

She wanted us to be like little children who possess nothing as their own and who depend entirely on their parents for all their needs. She urged us to live only from day to day without laying by any spiritual store for the future.

* * *

" If God should desire beautiful thoughts and sublime sentiments," she used to say, " He has His angels ! . . . Furthermore, He could have created human beings already perfect with none of the weaknesses of our nature. But no; He finds His delight in poor little weak and miserable creatures, like ourselves . . . Evidently, He derives greater pleasure from this choice."

Saint Thérèse had no difficulty in recalling texts and passages from Holy Scripture in order to strengthen her spiritual life. When I told her that I should like to be able to do that, too, but my memory was not good, she answered:

" There you go again, desiring riches and possessions ! To lean on these things is like leaning on a piece of red hot iron; it will always leave its little scar. We must lean on *nothing*, even in the case of those things which we have reason to believe might help us in the spiritual life. It is then that we are seeking only the truth which consists in having neither desire for nor hope of enjoyment. How happy we are when we have reached that stage. ' Where is the man,' asks the *Imitation*, ' that is wholly divested of all self-seeking? We must seek him from afar and from the uttermost coasts of the earth.' [2] From afar; that is, *very low* . . . very low in his own estimation, very low by reason of his humility; very low—in other words, somebody who is *very little* . . . "

* * *

She used to tell me, " You give yourself up too much to what you are doing, as though each duty were your last and that you were hoping that you had finally reached the end; then you are surprised when you stumble and fall. The truth is that you must always be expecting to fall.[3] You are concerned about the future as though it were your duty to provide for it. I sympathize with you in this for it is only natural for us to ask, ' O my God; what *fruits* shall I be able to offer you ? ' It is true that we all naturally

---

[2] *Imitation*, Book II, Chapter XI—4.

[3] In other words, that by this attitude of spiritual poverty, our falls may be profitable to our souls.

desire some tangible results from our efforts. ' Everybody seeketh a sign '; that is the way common to all. The only ones who do not seek a sign are those who are *poor in spirit* . . . "

*   *   *

I frequently manifested a desire that others should appreciate my efforts and take note of my spiritual progress.

" When you give in to this desire," the Saint admonished, " you are like the hen who, as soon as she has laid an egg, wants all the neighbours to know about it. Like her, the very moment you have performed a virtuous deed, or when you have acted from a very pure motive, everybody must know and praise you for it . . .

" How foolish of us," she went on to say, " to desire the esteem of some twenty nuns who live in the monastery with us—or to become disturbed in any way over any chance remarks they are liable to make. In their own little spheres, they are all more or less taken up with their personal interests and particular intentions; at one time they may be pre-occupied about their families or their own physical condition, and at another time, they are concerned about their spiritual progress. Even the saints, while they were on earth, were subject to these same limitations. Often when looking at their

pictures, I have been struck by the thought that
they, too, might have expressed themselves at
times in a very natural way, or even in a way
bordering on slang. It is then that I find myself
desiring to be loved and esteemed only in heaven
. . . for there alone shall we find the perfection
of love."

These sentiments were woven into the fabric
of Thérèse's daily life, for it was evident that on
earth she had asked to be accounted and esteemed
as nothing. How often she told me that " even
contempt " was too glorious for her, inasmuch as
" we can contemn only that which is known "—
whereas she yearned " to be *forgotten* entirely."

* * *

My dear little sister ardently desired that all
her acts of self-denial might remain hidden. I
had, on the contrary, frequent temptations to
vainglory, and was anxious, as I have already
said, that my praiseworthy actions should be
noticed. Thérèse used to tell me at such times:

> " You have learned the trade of *pushing self
> forward*. There are many who are in that
> business, I know, but I take care not to become
> involved in it because I am afraid I could not
> take in any profits. So I try, as far as possible,
> to hide what I do, and to deposit it all in the
> bank of the good God without bothering about
> the interest."

Once, when we were together, Thérèse laughingly took hold of my hand, printed in ink on my fingernail these words—*attachment to earthly goods*. She insisted that I remain branded in this way for some time.

* * *

It was my duty to keep the blankets of the monastery in good repair. One day when we were shaking them I asked rather sharply that they should be handled with greater care because they were already threadbare and worn. Saint Thérèse then said to me: " Suppose it were not your duty to mend these blankets? Then when you called attention to the fact that they are easily torn, you would do so impersonally, and then there would be no thought of self in the matter. In all your actions, try to avoid the least trace of self-seeking."

* * *

In an unpublished passage of her *Autobiography*, the Saint tells us about her visit, when she was twenty-eight months old, to the Visitation Convent at Le Mans, where, for the first time, she met her mother's sister, Sister Marie Dosithea.

In remembrance of the visit, the proud aunt gave the child a little beaded basket filled with candies, on the top of which were two sugar rings.

At once, the baby, overcome with happiness, cried out, " Oh ! how wonderful ! There is a sugar ring for Céline, too ! "

On her way to the station, however, when returning to Alençon, the basket overturned and, to her dismay, she saw her precious bonbons scattered along the street. Moreover, one of the coveted sugar rings had disappeared.

" Ah," sighed the little one, " I no longer have any sugar ring for poor Céline ! "

Years later, at Carmel, when reminding me of this incident, Thérèse made this observation: " See how deeply rooted in us is this self-love ! Why was it Céline's sugar ring, and not mine, that was lost? "

* * *

" Up to the age of fourteen," she confided to me, " I practised virtue without experiencing its sweetness, and I gathered in none of its fruits. My soul was like a beautiful tree, whose blossoms had scarcely opened when they fell . . . If God wills you also to have this experience, then offer up the sacrifice to Him: in other words, if He wills that throughout your entire life you should feel a repugnance to suffering and humiliation, if He permits all the flowers of your holy desires and good will to fall to the ground without any fruit, do not worry. At the moment of death, your soul will be laden with rich fruits which, at His Word, shall have fully ripened in the twinkling of an eye."

Our Lord showed me that Thérèse had judged wisely in this matter for I read later in the *Book of Ecclesiasticus* this passage, which delighted her when I told her about it:

> " There is an inactive man who wanteth help, is very weak in ability and full of poverty: yet the eye of the Lord hath looked upon him for good, and hath lifted him up from his low estate and hath exalted his head: and many have wondered at him and have glorified God . . . Trust in God and stay in thy place. For it is easy in the eyes of God on a sudden to make the poor man rich. The blessing of God maketh haste to reward the just, and in a swift hour His blessing beareth fruit." [4]

SPIRITUAL CHILDHOOD

When the Promoter of the Faith asked me at the Canonical Process, " Why do you desire the Beatification of Sister Thérèse of the Child Jesus? " I answered that it was solely that her Little Way *might become known to the world*. I spoke of it as a " Little Way " because the Saint had consistently used this expression when referring to that particular road along which she

---

[4] Eccl. XI, 12-13; 22-24.

was travelling to union with God. It was, what we might call, the symbol of her school of spirituality.

The Promoter of the Faith warned me, however, " Once you begin to speak of a special *Way*, the Cause is infallibly doomed; innumerable cases on record bear abundant witness to that."

" That is indeed too bad," I replied, " but a fear of hindering the Beatification of Sister Thérèse could never deter me from stressing the only important point that interests me—that her *Little Way* might be raised with her, so to speak, to the honours of the altar."

So I held out; nor did the Cause suffer as a result. In fact, everything relating to the Process began to move so rapidly that it was only a few years later that the decree on the heroicity of the virtues of Sister Thérèse was promulgated by the Sovereign Pontiff, Benedict XV. On that day, August 14, 1921, when His Holiness in his Discourse officially raised *The Way of Spiritual Childhood* to its exalted rank in the life of the Church, my joy reached heights never again attained, not even on those other memorable days later when my little sister Thérèse was first beatified and then canonized by Holy Mother Church.

The Acts of the Process also contains my answer to the question concerning the existence of any *extraordinary*, *spiritual phenomena* in the life of Thérèse.

"These were very rare in the life of the Servant of God," I replied. "For my part, I should prefer that she be not beatified if I could not portray the events of her life exactly as I judge them to be according to my conscience . . . Her life had, of necessity, to be very simple, in order to serve as a model for all *little souls*." [5]

Our dear Mistress was in the habit of meeting all our difficulties by pointing out the advantages of her *Little Way*. "In order to walk unfalteringly along this path," she was fond of repeating, "we must be *humble*, *simple* and *poor in spirit*."

How much she would have loved this prayer of Bossuet, had she known about it:

"Great God . . . Your desire is to enter our souls in a manner so simple as even to be shocking to some minds; by a door which, perhaps, is still too little known to them although from the early ages of the Church the saints have held it wide open. Grant, then, that none of these, of which some are wise and others spiritual, may be accused at Your dread Tribunal of having hindered in any way Your entrance into countless

---

[5] The Summarium, 2341, p. 799. We learn from other sources that Soeur Geneviève had to be very firm in this instance because another well-intentioned witness was endeavouring, during the Process, to emphasize the extraordinary element in the life of Saint Thérèse.

hearts because of the very simplicity of Your Approach. Grant, rather, that *becoming all like little children*, as Jesus Christ has commanded us, and having once for all entered by this little door, we may be thus enabled to point it out more surely and more efficaciously to others. Amen." [6]

It is not surprising to learn that in his last hours this great soul uttered these touching words:

> " If I could begin my life all over again, I should desire to remain ever as a very little child constantly reaching out for help from the Child Jesus."

* * *

Through that hidden wisdom which is revealed to little ones, Thérèse possessed a special faculty for discovering again this door to eternal life and of pointing it out to others. Her *Little Way* was, in practice, the virtue of *humility*. But it also established her, unmistakably in the *spirit of childhood*. She used to delight in pointing out to me various passages of the Gospel where there is reference to this spirit of childhood.

The following were some of her favourite quotations:

[6] Bossuet: *Manière courte et facile pour faire oraison.*

" Suffer the *little children* to come unto Me, for of such is the kingdom of heaven."—Cf. Matthew, XIX, 14.

" Their Angels always see the Face of My Father, Who is in heaven." Cf. Matthew XVIII, 10.

" Whosoever therefore shall humble himself as this little child, he is the greater in the kingdom of heaven." Cf. Matthew XVIII, 4.

" Jesus, after having embraced the little children, blessed them." Cf. Mark X, 16.

Thérèse had copied these sentences on the back of a picture of our four little brothers and sisters who died in infancy. She gave this memento to me and kept a duplicate in her breviary. Now yellow with age, the features of the little ones in the snapshot have, for the most part, been erased by the hand of time.

To these Gospel quotations she added texts drawn from Holy Writ, wherein the spirit of childhood is brought out in relief. She almost wept for joy whenever she came upon such passages like the following:

" Blessed is the man to whom God reputeth justice without works, for to him that worketh the reward is not reckoned according to grace but according to debt . . . It is, then (gratuitously) that he that worketh not is justified by grace in virtue of the redemption of Our Lord Jesus Christ." Cf. Romans IV, 4-6.

" The Lord shall feed his flock like a shepherd. He shall gather together the *little lambs*, and shall take them up in his bosom." Cf. Isaias XL, 11.

Soeur Thérèse wrote out some scriptural texts on another card also. Although several of these quotations are merely repetitions of those I have already listed, I shall give them here as it is interesting to see how much they influenced the Saint as she progressed along her *Little Way*.

" Whosoever is a little one, let him come to Me." Cf. Proverbs IX, 4.

" Whosoever therefore shall humble himself as a little child he is greater in the kingdom of heaven." Cf. Matthew XVIII, 4.

" The Lord shall gather together the *little lambs*, and shall take them up in his bosom." Cf. Isaias XL, 11.

" As one whom a mother caresseth, so will I comfort you . . . I shall carry you at my breast and on my knee I shall caress you." Cf. Isaias LXVI, 12-13.

" As a father hath compassion on his children, so hath the Lord compassion on us . . . As far as the east is from the west, so far hath He removed our iniquities from us . . . The Lord is compassionate and full of mercy, long-suffering and plenteous in mercy." Cf. Psalms CII, 13-12-8.

"He that doeth the will of my Father is my sister, my brother and my mother . . ." Cf. Luke XII, 50.

"Father, those whom you have given me, you have loved them as you have also loved me." Cf. John XVII, 23.

Another one of her treasures was a picture of a child on Our Lord's knees, trying his best to reach up to kiss His Face. On one occasion, when I showed her a memorial card with a picture of a baby who had just died, she passed her hand over the little one's face and exclaimed with tenderness and holy pride, "They all belong to my kingdom." Even then it seemed that she knew that some day she would be called, "Reine des Tout-Petits." [7]

Soeur Thérèse was rather tall, about five-foot-four, whereas Mère Agnès (our sister) was very short. One day, when I asked Thérèse whether—if she had her choice—she would prefer to be short or tall, she answered unhesitatingly, "I should prefer to be short in order to be *little* in every way."

* * *

In the mind of the Church, Saint Thérèse of the Child Jesus has always been the Saint of

---

[7] Queen of the very Little Ones, not, it is to be noted "Tous-Petits" but "Tout," very little.

Spiritual Childhood. Several Pontiffs have borne unimpeachable testimony to this. However, I shall limit myself here to a quotation of the Sovereign Pontiff Pius XII, now gloriously reigning. As Cardinal Pacelli, the legate *a latere* of Pius XI for the inauguration of the Basilica at Lisieux, July 11, 1937, His Eminence said:

> " Saint Thérèse of the Child Jesus has a mission, a doctrine. But like everything else about this Carmelite Saint, her doctrine is humble and simple and it is summed up in these two words: *Spiritual Childhood*—or in their equivalent: *The Little Way*."

Not only Divine, but also human wisdom has discerned in this *spirit of childhood* our *true grandeur of soul*. Even before the Christian era, there were pagan philosophers who had subscribed to this belief, as we see from the following quotations:

In the sixth century B.C. Lao-tse said, " Mature virtue is perfected in the spirit of childhood." [8] And again, " To be virile in the practice of virtue is always to advance along the right way and to return to the spirit of childhood." [9]

---

[8] Quoted by John C. H. Wu, in his work entitled: *Dom Lou, Sa Vie Spirituelle*, p. 41, Desclee de Brouwer 1949.

[9] Tao-Teh-Ching quoted by John C. H. Wu in his brochure *La Science de l'Amour*, p. 29.

Mancius wrote in the fourth century B.C., "The great man is he who has not lost the heart of a child." [10]

* * *

Soeur Thérèse kept March 25th each year as a day of special devotion. It was the Feast of the Incarnation and, as she used to tell us, the Infant Jesus, in the bosom of Mary, was never as small as He was on that day.

But it was the Mystery of the Infant Jesus in the Crib at Bethlehem that was her special delight, for it was there that He was in the habit of whispering to her all His secrets about simplicity and abandonment. In contrast to the heresiarch Marcion who disdainfully cried, "Away with these swaddling bands and with this crib, so unworthy of a God!", Thérèse was entranced at the thought of the abasement of Our Lord in becoming so *little* for the love of us. On the Nativity pictures which she used to paint, she was always happy to print this sentence of Saint Bernard: "Jesus, what made You become so little?—LOVE."

---

[10] Quoted together with the words of Mancius in *Dom Lou*, p. 41.
Doctor John C. H. Wu, former Chinese Ambassador to the Holy See, is also the author of *Beyond East and West* and *The Interior Carmel*—Sheed and Ward, N.Y. Saint Thérèse had a major rôle in Doctor Wu's conversion which he describes in moving terms in the story of his life, *Beyond East and West*.

The name *Thérèse de l'Enfant Jésus* which had been promised to her at the age of nine when she expressed a desire to become a Carmelite during her visit with the Prioress, Mère Marie de Gonzague, had a definite meaning for her and she constantly endeavoured to become worthy of it. Later on, she composed this prayer: " O Jesus, dear Holy Child, my only Treasure, I abandon myself to Thy Divine *whims*. I seek no other joy than that of calling forth Thy sweet smile. Imprint Thy grace upon my soul and the virtues of Thy Holy Childhood, so that on the day of my birth into heaven the Angels and Saints may recognize Thérèse of the Child Jesus in Thy little spouse."

I might add that these virtues of *spiritual childhood*, long before the time of Thérèse, had, we are told, won the admiration of the austere Saint Jerome—certainly an endorsement, if any endorsement be needed, of the virile spirituality of the *Little Way*.

* * *

" There are great saints who have *won* Heaven by their works," Thérèse said one day, " but my favourite patrons are those who *stole* it—like the Holy Innocents and the Good Thief. I want to imitate these thieves and win Heaven by stratagem, a stratagem of love which will open its gates to me and to all poor sinners with me. The Holy Ghost encourages me with the words 'Come to me, little one, to learn subtlety.'"[11]

I questioned Thérèse about the penances performed by the Saints.

"Our Lord assured us," she replied, "that in His Father's House there are many mansions . . . If every soul called to perfection were obliged to perform these austerities in order to enter heaven, Our Lord would have given us some clear indication of it and we would respond eagerly. But He Himself has declared, 'In My Father's House there are many mansions.'[12] If, then, there are mansions set apart for great souls, for the Fathers of the desert and for the martyrs of penance, there must also be one for *little children*. So a place is waiting for us there if we but love Him dearly together with Our Heavenly Father and the Spirit of Love."

Soeur Thérèse was a simple soul who became a saint by making use of the ordinary means of sanctification. This is one of the chief reasons why she proves to be such an excellent model for all *little souls*. If on the other hand extraordinary gifts of grace had been more in evidence in her life they might have interfered with God's special designs on her soul.

---

[11] Proverbs I:4.
[12] John XIV-2.

Once I said to her, " What would you do if you could begin your religious life all over again? " " It seems to me that I should do just as I have done," Thérèse answered. " Then you do not agree with the hermit who said that although he had spent long years in penance, until his very last breath he would fear to be damned." " Indeed I do not agree with him, for I am too small to lose my soul," Thérèse assured me: " Little children do not damn themselves."

* * *

In a discouraged mood I went one day to Thérèse for help and told her: " This time it is impossible. I simply cannot rise above this trial." " This does not surprise me," she replied, " for we are too small to *rise above* our difficulties. Therefore let us try to pass under them."

To illustrate this point she recalled a childhood experience we had shared together. We were visiting the Lehoux family in Alençon and wanted to play in the garden but we could not get in because a horse blocked the entrance.

" While the older girls were trying to find some way to pass the horse," Thérèse said, " our little playmate Thérèse Lehoux [13] discovered that the easiest way to get by was to go *under* the horse. She slipped through first, holding my

---

[13] A playmate who, like Céline, was then seven years old.

hand. I followed, pushing her a little as we went along. We were both so small that we scarcely had to bend at all in order to go under the horse, and we were in the garden in a short time. That is the advantage of staying small. There are no obstacles for little ones; they can slip in unnoticed everywhere."

" Great souls," said Thérèse, " can rise above their trials. They can surmount human obstacles, either by reasoning things out or through the practice of virtue. But in our case, because we are so little, we must never attempt to use such means. Let us, rather, always pass *under* our difficulties. In other words, let us not reason too much about our human affairs; we should not consider them at very close range." [14]

* * *

During her illness Thérèse used to take the most disagreeable remedies with angelic patience and submit to other painful treatments without any complaint. Although she knew, and repeated to us several times, that, for her, medical care was to no purpose, she made no objection what-

---

[14] At the time, Thérèse's novices had no responsibility, strictly speaking, to treat of human affairs. Their duty as novices was to remain disentangled from all earthly concern. To those whose office it is to battle with problems of life and to make decisions, Thérèse would qualify her counsel by urging those in charge not to waste time in *useless* reasoning or calculations of the difficulties.

ever to all the pain and fatigue that came to her because of these medications. She told me in confidence that she was offering to God all those " useless " remedies, and asking that some poor missionary who had neither time nor means to take care of himself might profit by her offering.

As I did not experience any beautiful sentiments of this kind, I said so, with regrets.

" Such an explicit intention is not at all necessary for a soul that is entirely given over to God." Thérèse answered. " The infant at the mother's breast takes its nourishment as a matter of course, and without giving a thought to the reason for the action. Yet he thrives on it and it gives him strength and vitality, even though that is not his intention while feeding at the breast.

" An artist at work for his master does not need to repeat, with each stroke of the brush, ' I am working for Mr. X; this is for Mr. X.' No; it is enough for him to apply himself to his work assiduously, and with the intention and the will to do it all for his master. Undoubtedly, it is commendable to recollect our thoughts frequently, and to direct our intention from time to time, but with nothing like constraint. Almighty God knows very well all the beautiful thoughts and ingenious expressions of love we should like to have, for He is our Father and we are His little children."

One day I said to her, " I must do my work or I'll make Jesus sad." "Indeed not," she countered. " It is you who will become sad. The involuntary faulty actions and omissions of those in the *Little Way* do not sadden Him. But how miserable *we* shall be if we do not give Him all that it is possible to give."

*   *   *

Because she was profoundly humble, Thérèse believed herself " incapable of climbing the rugged ladder of perfection." She turned her thoughts rather to the art of becoming smaller and smaller so that God would accept full responsibility for her. He would treat her as all babies are treated. He would *carry her in His Arms.* She yearned to become a saint, but without growing up. For, she believed, that just as the clumsiness of little ones does not offend their parents, neither would her imperfections be distressing to Our Lord. She was trusting implicitly in God's holy indulgence toward all little souls, for " to him that is little, mercy is granted." [15]

With this point of view, Soeur Thérèse was able to resist any thought that she might have reached perfection. She did not want others to think that she was perfect, for that would mean

[15] Wisdom, VI-7.

that she had grown up and in that case God would
expect her to go her way alone. She used to say,
" Children do not work in order to make a name
for themselves; no, they work only to make their
parents happy. Like devoted and loving children,
we should practise virtue, not to become saints
but to *please Almighty God*."

* * *

One day, during Thérèse's illness, I had
shown a lack of virtue and was bitterly repenting
the fault.

" Kiss your crucifix," said Thérèse. I obeyed,
kissing the feet. " Is that how a child kisses her
father?" she exclaimed. " Kiss His Face." I did
so, and then, following her request that I have
Him return my caress, I tenderly pressed the
crucifix to my cheek.

" Now," Thérèse said quietly, " all is forgiven."

* * *

On another occasion Thérèse was telling me
how Our Lord had said to the mother of the sons
of Zebedee, " To sit on My right or left hand
is not Mine to give you but to them for whom
it is prepared by my Father." [16] " *I somehow feel*,"
she commented, " *that these special thrones refused*

---

[16] Matthew, XX-23.

to the great saints and martyrs are reserved for little
children . . . David foretold this in the Psalms,
singing, ' . . . little Benjamin will preside
amidst the assemblies (of the saints).' " [17]

When I asked her, then, by what name we
might pray to her in heaven, she replied
humbly, " Call me *little* Thérèse."

CONFIDENCE

Thérèse was inexhaustible when her conversations and conferences had to do with God's
mercy and love.   As she tells us in her *Autobiography*, in her childhood and early youth
she had ardently desired to become " a saint
and a great saint."   But, as the years went
on, her confidence was to become so daring that
even the most extravagant hopes did not seem
beyond realization.   This confidence grew from
her ambition to lose herself entirely in the
infinite riches of the merits of Jesus.   " The
treasures of His Merits are mine," she wrote in
her Act of Oblation.   She was always telling us
that we can never desire too much nor ask too
much when we are asking of God.

" Some people in life know how to ingratiate
themselves into everyone's affection," she said.
" They know how to obtain all they desire . . .
So when we importune God for something He
had not intended to give us, He gives it, for He

---

[17] Cf. Psalms, LXVII-28.

is powerful and rich and will not let us be disappointed . . . "

Soeur Thérèse never employed this means in her own case when there was need only for consolation or for the alleviation of pain. She was circumspect about asking for favours in the temporal order.

Believing that God would refuse her nothing, she was careful about what she asked for, " because," she naïvely remarked, " He might feel obliged to hear me favourably."

Whenever she did ask for relief or some other temporal favour, it was only to please others. Even then, she would make sure to ask through the Blessed Virgin because " to ask through the Blessed Virgin is not the same as asking directly from the good God. She knows very well how to take care of my little desires and whether or not to mention them to God . . . I leave it to her to see that He shall not be forced, so to speak, to grant my prayers, but rather that He be left entirely free to do His Will in all that concerns me."

When she expressed her desire " to do good on earth " after her death, it was only on condition that " I shall first make sure to look well into the eyes of God so that I may not ask any favour that is contrary to His Will."

The Saint was encouraged to use this form of prayer by the remembrance of the simple

petition of Our Lady at Cana, " They have no
wine," [18] and that of Martha and Mary of
Bethany, " He whom Thou lovest is sick." [19]   In
each case, the desire alone was revealed.   No
formal request was made, and Jesus was free to
do whatever He willed in the matter.

* * *

Although her *Little Way*, the *Way of Spiritual
Childhood*, is a way of blind and complete confidence, Thérèse was far from minimizing the
rôle of *personal co-operation* in the matter of our
sanctification.   She was always emphasizing this
point in her instructions to us in the novitiate.
There could be no better proof of the importance
she attached to this idea than the example of her
own spiritual life: it was one long series of
generous and consistent acts of virtue.

I had been struck by the passage in *Ecclesiasticus*,
" All mercy shall make a place for every man
according to the merit of his works, and according to the wisdom of his sojournment." [20]
Discussing this with Thérèse I said that I thought
she had directed the course of her life with a
wisdom that was sublime; consequently, a very
special place must be reserved in heaven for her.

---

[18] John II-3.
[19] John XVI-15.
[20] Eccl. XVI-15.

The phrase " according to his works," however bothered me.

Spiritedly Thérèse explained that confidence in God and the virtue of abandonment are nourished only by sacrifice. " We must do all in our power," she said, " to give without counting and to deny ourselves constantly. We must prove our love by all the good works of which we are capable and which, after all, are of little worth . . . Even when we have done all that we think should be done, we are to consider ourselves ' unprofitable servants,' [21] hoping at the same time that God will, through His grace, give us all that we desire. This is what all little souls who *run* in the way of spiritual childhood should hope for." "Remember," she reminded me, " I say *run*, not *rest*."

* * *

My beloved little sister tried at all times to instil in my heart the desire, the humble confidence which possessed her own heart, to be spared consignment to Purgatory hereafter. This hope soon became for me, like the air. the atmosphere in which I breathed.

On Christmas night 1894, while still a postulant, I found hidden in my slipper a note with some verses which Thérèse had written for

[21] Luke XVII-10.

me in the name of Our Lady. The concluding verses bear on this subject:

> Jesus Himself your crown shall weave
> And if you seek His Love alone,
> If all for Him you gladly leave
> Near His, some day, shall be your throne.

> After the night of life, the day
> With light eternal shining through
> You shall behold ! *With no delay*
> *The Triune God shall welcome you !*

In her Act of Oblation to the merciful love of God, Thérèse closes with this petition:

> " . . . May this martyrdom, after having prepared me to appear before Thee, finally cause my death, and then may *my soul take its flight without delay* into the eternal embrace of Thy Merciful Love . . . "

In the words of Saint John of the Cross— " The more God wishes to bestow on us, the more does He make us desire "—she found justification for her own unbounded desires, as also her hope for their realization.

It was her spirit of Abandonment and Love that made her hope to escape the fires of Purgatory. The virtue of humility, so dear to her heart and so characteristic of childhood, gave her still another motive for this hope; the child truly loves his parents and, since he is powerless and weak, he had no other thought than to abandon himself to them entirely.

" Can a father scold his child when the child is the first to own up to his fault? " she used to say. " Certainly not. He just presses the little one to his heart."

To illustrate her point, she recounted a story we had read in our childhood.

A king who had set out on the chase noticed his dogs pursuing a white rabbit which was a little ahead of them. When the little rabbit began to sense that the dogs were about to pounce upon him, turning suddenly around, he bounded back quickly and jumped up into the arms of the huntsman. Deeply moved by this show of confidence, the king cherished the rabbit thereafter as his own; he allowed no one to molest him and nourished and cared for the little animal himself.

" This is how God will treat us," Thérèse added, " if, when hunted down by the claims of Divine Justice, represented by the little dogs in the story, we run for refuge into the very arms of our Judge . . . "

Here, of course, she had in mind those little souls who walk in the Way of Spiritual Childhood, but she held out the very same hope even for the worst sinners on earth. It was for such as these that she wrote in her *Autobiography*:

" Ah ! I am certain that even if I had on my conscience every imaginable crime, I should lose nothing of my confidence; rather would I hasten, with a heart broken with sorrow, to throw myself into the Arms of my Jesus. I remember how He cherished the prodigal son who had returned to Him. It is not because the good God in His *preventing* love and mercy has preserved me from mortal sin that I lift up my heart to Him in confidence and love . . . " [22]

* * *

When I entered Carmel, I began almost immediately to read the Lives of the Fathers of the Desert.[23] I took some notes as I read and one of the stories that I copied impressed Thérèse very deeply. She regretted that she had not included it in the manuscript of her *Life* and entreated us to do so later. This is the story:

A sinner named Paésie had scandalized the whole town by her evil life, and a Father of the desert, John the Dwarf, went in search of her to impress upon her the need of penance and reparation. At last, realizing the enormity of her sins, she asked, " Is there any penance that could possibly make amends for my wicked life? If there is, then send me wheresoever you will

[22] From the original manuscript of Saint Thérèse's *Autobiography*, Ms. C., fol. 36v.

[23] *Vie des Pire des Désert d'Orient*, par R.P. Michel-Ange Marin.

that I might perform it." When the hermit had reassured her, she rose up at once, and telling no one else her purpose nor even settling any of her affairs, she followed the holy man into the desert.

Arriving at nightfall, John made a pillow of sand and, marking it with the Sign of the Cross, he told Paésie to rest her head there for the night. Moving a little distance away, he too—after he had prayed—stretched himself out in the sand and went to sleep. But at midnight he was startled by a stream of light which, coming down from heaven, rested on Paésie. And in that light he beheld the angels bearing the soul of the penitent up to heaven. At the same time, he heard these miraculous words:

" Her penance, of only a few hours duration has pleased God more because of her intense love than the long penitential lives of many others whose love did not measure up to hers."

Soeur Thérèse often repeated to me that the justice of God is satisfied with very little when *love* is the motive of our reparation; even then He mitigates, to an excessive degree, the *temporal* punishment due to sin, for He is gentleness itself.

" I have frequently noticed," she confided to me, " that after I have committed a fault, even a slight one, my soul experiences a certain sadness or uneasiness for some little time. Then I tell myself, ' Now, little one, this is the price you must pay for your fault,' and so I patiently bear with the trial until the little debt is paid."

According to her understanding of the virtue of hope, that was the extent of satisfaction required by Divine Justice for those who are humble and who abandon themselves to God in love. She could not believe such souls would have to go to Purgatory. She thought, rather, that at the moment of death their Father in heaven, because of their confidence, would kindle in their souls as they realized their misery an attitude of perfect contrition, and that in this way their entire debt should be cancelled.

Celine (left) at age 12 with her sister St. Thérèse at age 8.
(Photo taken in 1881.)

St. Thérèse at age 15 (1888), shortly before her entry into Carmel.

Office Central de Lisieux

St. Thérèse in July of 1896, at age 23.

St. Thérèse (left) in the laundry with her sister Celine—Sister Geneviève of the Holy Face—in the year 1895.

St. Thérèse (holding hourglass) and her novices, with Reverend Mother Agnes of Jesus (standing tallest in the window) and Mother Mary Gonzaga (also standing in the window). Standing on the far right is Sister Geneviève of the Holy Face (Celine).

St. Thérèse with her sisters and cousin. Top left: Sister Marie of the Sacred Heart (Marie). Top right: Sister Geneviève of the Holy Face (Celine). Middle row, left: Rev. Mother Agnes of Jesus (Pauline). Middle row, right: St. Thérèse of the Child Jesus. Front: Sister Marie of the Blessed Sacrament (Marie Guérin).

CHAPTER III

LOVE OF GOD

MANY of the great mystics, in order to attain to the perfection of love, exercised themselves continuously in the practice of the Christian virtues. But that was not Saint Thérèse's method either in theory or in practice. Although unitive love was the burning ideal of her life, that same love was also the underlying principle of all her actions. Whatever the form of her human activity, primarily she was always interiorly engaged in loving God. In this way she reached the summit of divine love in the space of a few years. She tells us something about it in these words:

" I know that it was for the glory of God that the great saints laboured and suffered, but as one of His very little souls I live for His pleasure alone, to gratify the divine ' fancies,' so to speak. I would willingly undergo the greatest sufferings (even, if this were possible, without His being aware of them) not in view of any accidental glory He might derive from them— no, that would be too much !—but simply to make Him smile, even once . . . Multitudes there are who yearn to be *useful* ! But my one ambition is to remain as a *worthless* toy in the hands of the Child Jesus . . . to become one with the ' whims ' of the Divine Infant ! . . . " [1]

* * *

It was during her last illness that the Saint said to me one day: " My chief desire through life has been *to give pleasure to the good God.* How sorely tempted to discouragement I should be at present had it been otherwise—if, for instance, I had been intent on storing up merit for myself."

It was evident that Thérèse in her deep humility made no account of all her good works. She loved to recall that even our works of justice are full of blemish in the sight of God. As death approached, therefore, she was dwelling only on the love that had motivated her actions during life.

* * *

" The good God Who loves us so much," our Saint exclaimed one day, " has sorrow enough in being obliged to leave us on earth to fill out

---

[1] " . . . moi, je suis un *caprice* du petit Jésus . . . " *Caprice*, italicized in the French edition, was used in this sense in Saint Thérèse's time. The expression is now considered obsolete. The statement (in a recent publication) that the Saint here used the word " caprice " in the sense of " freak " is without any foundation. (Tr.).

our time of probation without our constantly reminding Him that we are miserable down here. On our part we should act as though we were not conscious of our sufferings."

It was clear that Thérèse moved easily about in this atmosphere of *love* which was the dominant note of her life and teaching. It was, for example, " only by stealth " that she wiped the excessive perspiration from her face in the burning heat of summer or rubbed her hands together in the cold Normandy winters. Acting in this way, as she put it so naïvely, " would not give God time to notice " her sufferings . . .

Likewise, in her early religious life, when practising a Carmelite penance which was particularly difficult for her at the time, " I used to force myself to *smile*," she confided to us later, " in order that God, as though *deceived* by my countenance, should not suspect that I was suffering."

Again, in her own inimitable way, she told us: " If the joys of heaven should not come up to my expectations, I shall be careful not to let this be seen. Then the good God will not be aware of my disappointment ! . . . "

* * *

I told Thérèse of my distress that I could not imitate her in her refinements of the love of

God . . . " Do you believe," I asked, " that my ardent *desires* to love Him in this way will suffice? "

" Most assuredly," she answered with animation, " especially if you will accept your limitations in the matter with humility. Moreover, if you will go a step further and rejoice over it, you may please Jesus more than if you were always experiencing great sweetness in your spiritual life. When bereft of such consolations, it would be well to say this prayer:

' I am grateful, O my God, that you do not permit me to experience any tender feeling whatever in my union with you. I am happy, nevertheless, to witness the tangible effects of such delicate tenderness in others . . . *For thou hast given me, O Lord, a delight in thy doings.*'"[2]

* * *

The burning flame of love which was consuming Thérèse's soul was continually being fed by the fuel of self-sacrifice. With jealous care she kept her heart entirely disengaged from all created things. I had a fine example of this one day, when both of us happened to be standing before a bookcase, and Thérèse gaily exclaimed, " Oh ! how sorry I should now be had I read

---

[2] Ps. XCI, 5.

all those books ! " [3] Rather surprised, I replied: " I don't understand. I could readily understand your regret at the prospect of having *to read them all in the future*. But if that labour *were already behind you*, would it not be to your advantage to have absorbed so much spiritual doctrine? " " Had I read them all," the Saint rejoined, " I should have only broken my poor little head and have lost the precious time which I have spent, instead, in loving God."

* * *

GENEROSITY

I mentioned to my dear little Mistress one day that, apparently, God was wont to ask more of me than He required of other souls. I saw that I was called upon to renounce some legitimate pleasures which other sisters could enjoy in peace. Thérèse took me up on this and said:

" As for me, I do not concern myself about what God might be asking of others; nor do I assume that I store up greater merit when I am obliged to sacrifice more than other souls in His service. Whatever He asks of me always makes me happy. Furthermore, if I were allowed to have a preference, which is impossible, I should always choose precisely that which He wills for me. It is because of this attitude of

---

[3] " Oh ! que je serais *marrie* d'avoir lu " etc.

mind that I find my lot in life a beautiful one. Even if others merited more in giving less, I should desire for myself less merit in giving Him more, simply because that would be His Holy Will for me."

And when I told her that she seemed to be very happy over the thought of going soon to join Our Lord in heaven, she replied:

"It is certainly not for my own happiness that I desire to go to Him, for my attraction for suffering is much more intense than my desire for heaven. I am welcoming death now only because I know it is God's will for me; otherwise, I should desire, rather, to live on— and then die a martyr in the end."

* * *

Although it grieved her whenever she heard that some other religious communities were undergoing persecution, the possibility that we also might be called upon some day to shed our blood for Christ always fired her soul with holy enthusiasm. At such times, her glowing words gave abundant proof of the love that was consuming her magnanimous heart. One day, during her last illness, I heard her sigh, "To think that I am actually going to die in bed when I have always had such a longing to go out and meet death in some arena!"

Certain persons,[4] judging that it was beyond his means, criticized my father for his gift of a new high-altar to the Cathedral of Saint Pierre, our parish church in Lisieux. The inference was that he had done an injustice to his two daughters who were still living in the world. Thérèse, on the other hand, was jubilant over the gift, and made this remark at the time:

> " It is only to be expected that, having given all his children to God, he should now provide an altar for their immolation, and for his own."

* * *

I had confided to the Saint that at the recitation of the Divine Office one night I had found devotion in simply offering to the Divine Majesty, at intervals, some fragrant flowers from the abundant store with which nature has endowed us. At the alternate verses of the Office I would choose from my spiritual garden some new spray of flowers—roses, lilies and the endless varieties that appeal to me—and then offer it to God during the next psalm. When I

---

[4] When at Mass, one Sunday in 1888, it was announced from the pulpit that 10,000 francs would defray the cost of a new altar, Thérèse's father donated the sum at once. It was to be considered an *anonymous* bequest but the Saint's uncle, Isidore Guérin, had to be informed of what was considered the " improvident " gift of his brother-in-law.

had plucked the last flower and the garden was bare, I told her, I began to consider the possibilities offered by some fruit trees a short distance away. After but a moment's hesitation, I proceeded to rifle the trees of their blossoms—the apple-trees, the apricot and the cherry-trees—and at the last prayer of the Office, having plundered the garden of all its treasures, I was happy in the thought that I had given God everything and had held nothing back.

This novel kind of offering delighted my beloved Thérèse, and she took the occasion to enunciate to me the properties of love. It belongs to love *to sacrifice everything*, she told me, to give generously, to become a spendthrift, to act with folly. Love is prodigal to excess, she continued, and never counts the cost; love knows not how to calculate and freely foregoes all hope of any dividends. " Oh ! happy recklessness ! Oh ! blessed intoxication of love !" she cried. " Oh ! for that love which gives all with the total surrender of self besides ! Nevertheless, with many of us how often is it only after the greatest deliberation that we finally give way; how loath we are to sacrifice our temporal advantages and our spiritual interests. Does this deserve the name of love? No, for love is blind; it is a torrent that rapidly sweeps up everything in its train."

* * *

On another occasion I told her I was full of holy envy whenever I considered the special talents God had given her and which she was using to such great advantage to win other souls to Him. " I should be so happy," I added, " if I, too, could compose beautiful poems to inspire others with the love of God." Thérèse replied:

" We should become utterly detached from such things, and not set our hearts on doing good to others by means of poetry, art, or by literary works . . . Oh no ! When faced by our limitations, we must have recourse to the practice of offering to God the good works of others. That is the advantage of the Communion of Saints. Let us never grieve over our powerlessness but rather apply ourselves solely to the science of love." After giving me a thought from Tauler [5] on the subject, she continued: " We are told that the love uniting all the elect in heaven is so great and so pure that the happiness and merit of each individual saint makes for the happiness and merit of all; as though each one were constantly enjoying

[5] " If I love the good that is in my neighbour more than he himself loves it, this good becomes mine more than it is his. If, for instance, in Saint Paul, I love all the favours God bestowed on him, all these, by the same title belong to me. Through this communion, I can become enriched by all the good that is in heaven and upon earth, in the angels and in the saints; in a word, by all the good in everyone who loves God." Sermons of Tauler— sermon for 5th Sunday after Blessed Trinity Feast.

and participating in the merits of all the other blessed inhabitants there." [6]

" So as you see," the Saint concluded, " by your *desire* to accomplish such good, and by lovingly exercising yourself in the practice of the most hidden virtue, you will do as much good as I, and even more; if, for example, *you render a service which may be slight in itself but which costs you very much.* You know well," she added, " how poor I am myself, but the good God *measures out* to me just what I need at each moment."

* * *

During the winter of 1896-1897, in order to protect Thérèse's feet from the cold, Mère Marie de Gonzague, our Prioress, gave her an order of obedience to use a foot-warmer. This would enable my little sister who was already in a decline to have a warm pair of alpargates [7] always at hand. But the Saint never used this dispensation unless the necessity was great—and

---

[6] " Even in heaven each one will rejoice in the goods of the others." Cf. Saint Thomas, S.T. Supplement, Question 71, art. 1.

The following passage from Abbé Arminjon's work, entitled: *Fin du monde present et mystères de la vie future* bears on this subject: " Among all the elect there will be but one heart . . . the eternal riches of one will be the eternal riches of all; each heart will vibrate with the happiness of all other hearts in heaven." (7th Conference: *De la beatitude eternelle de la vision surnaturelle de Dieu*). The Abbé's work had a particular attraction for Saint Thérèse.

[7] Sandals worn by Carmelite nuns.

even then, only because it was Reverend Mother's wish.

Consequently, except when she was unusually chilled, Thérèse allowed the foot-warmer to cool off, much to my evident displeasure. " Other souls, at death," she observed in her light-hearted way, " present themselves before the heavenly court weighted down by their in-struments of penance, whereas I shall appear there holding up *ma chaufferette*.[8] Never mind, it is only love and obedience that count . . . "

* * *

To prove that God looks only to the love which inspires our actions, one day Soeur Thérèse related the following story to us:

> " Once there was a great lord who built a church in his realm as a lasting memorial to his liberality. On the day of the grand dedication, this sovereign's name and the name of his family could be clearly seen, carved in bold letters on one of the prominent stones of the building. The next day, however, the only name to be seen on the stone was that of some unknown woman. Needless to say, the original inscription, which had been completely obliterated, was restored at once, but the same phenomenon again took place. After several renewed

---

[8] The foot-warmer.

attempts to by-pass the miracle were similarly frustrated, the irate lord began an investigation. He had at the outset forbidden his subjects to contribute, even in a small way, to this project; *he* was to be the sole donor. Now he began to suspect that somebody had secretly interfered with his plan. The unknown name was, therefore, duly identified, and the guilty woman summoned to justice. Denying, at first, all responsibility in the matter, she suddenly remembered . . . During the building operations, she had noticed how difficult it was for the horses to drag along the heavy cartloads of stone, and with her last coin, she had bought a truss of hay for them. ' These dumb animals are, in a certain way, participating in this great work,' she had reasoned, ' and as I have been deprived of the privilege of contributing directly to this temple, perhaps God will accept the offering I am making through them . . . ' That was the extent of her guilt. The humbled sovereign fully understood . . . and there was no further interference with the miraculous inscription."

" This proves," Thérèse added, " that the most trivial work, the least action when inspired by love, is often of greater merit than the most outstanding achievement. It is not on their face value that God judges our deeds, even when they bear the stamp of apparent holiness, but solely on the measure of love we put into them . . . And there is no one," she concluded, " who can object that he is incapable of even this much, for such love is within the reach of all men."

* * *

One day when we were conversing together, Thérèse said: " You remember that beautiful stanza in the *Spiritual Canticle* of our holy Father, Saint John of the Cross, which begins:

' Return, thou dove,
For the wounded hart
Appears on the hill
At the air of the flight and takes
refreshment. '

" Well, the Spouse, the *wounded Hart*, is not attracted," she went on to say, " by *the grandeur* of the hills (the image of our spectacular actions), but only by the *air* of the flight. And to think that one single movement of the dove's wings— such as a simple act of genuine charity—is sufficient to create this breeze of love."

* * *

In our childhood, the kaleidoscope was one of our favourite amusements. [9]

---

[9] A small telescope or spy-glass. As the instrument revolves there is an endless variety of colour visible to the peering eye.

" This toy," Thérèse told me later when we were in Carmel, " intrigued me, and for a long time I kept wondering just what could produce so delightful a phenomenon. One day a careful examination revealed that the unusual effect was merely the result of a combination of tiny scraps of paper and bits of wool (of no special form) scattered about inside. When on further scrutiny I discovered three looking-glasses inside the tube, the puzzle was solved. And this simple toy became for me the image of a great mystery." The Saint then made this apt comparison:

" So long as our actions, even the most trivial, remain within love's kaleidoscope, the Blessed Trinity (which the three converging glasses represent) imparts to them a marvellous brightness and beauty. Yes, so long as love is in our heart and we do not withdraw from our centre, *all is well*.[10] Saint John of the Cross tells us, ' Love knows how to draw profit from all, from the good as well as from the evil it finds in us, which evil it transforms, together with all things, into itself.'[11]

" The eye-piece of the spy-glass symbolizes the good God, who, looking from outside (but through Himself, as it were) into the *kaleidoscope* finds everything quite beautiful, even our miserable straws of effort and our most insignificant actions. But, just let us withdraw from

[10] Isaias, III, 10.

[11] From Saint John of the Cross's " Gloss on the Divine."

our centre, and then His divine Eye would behold nothing but the scattered atoms of our worthless actions."

* * *

Thérèse often repeated that she did not want her spiritual life to resemble the traffic-life of a street-vendor, whose trade yields little or no profit. " Notwithstanding, there are some souls," she would add, " who are really satisfied to gain their spiritual livelihood in bartering like that over a little counter and earning a mere pittance in return. But I prefer," she continued, " *to speculate in the Bank of Love* . . . and there I bid for high stakes. If I lose in this business of mine, I soon find out about it. I am not at all concerned, however, with financial matters, because Jesus takes care of all that for me. Actually, I do not even know if I am rich or poor. But some day I shall indeed know."

* * *

One day, bringing the Epistles of Saint Paul to me, Thérèse exclaimed with great enthusiasm:

" Listen to what the Apostle says:

' For it is not to a mountain that might be touched that you are come (through love) nor a burning fire, nor a whirlwind . . . but to the

> mountain of Sion, and to the city of the living God, the heavenly Jerusalem, and to the company of many thousands of angels, and to the church of the first-born . . . *for our God is a consuming fire.*' " [12]

And repeating this last sentence, she developed the theme with much feeling.

HER ACT OF OBLATION [13]

Saint Thérèse of the Child Jesus possessed profound insight into the mystery of the Divine Paternity, and the underlying theme of all her instructions to the novices was that of the ineffable riches of the Merciful Love of God. She delighted in pointing out to us that it is the Fatherhood of God that impels Him to forgive His children's offences.   If we will abandon ourselves to Him with absolute confidence in His Goodness, He will hasten to our aid and, drawing us closer to His Heart, will pour His abundant graces upon us.

Thérèse saw, on the one hand, that among the friends of God, there are those chosen souls

---

[12] Cf. Heb. XII, 18, 22, 23, 29.

[13] For those readers who are not familiar with the Thérèsian *Act of Oblation*, Sister Geneviève's penetrating analysis will be of service here.

In her *Conseils et Souvenirs*, this commentary on the fundamental meaning of this *Act* is given only as an Appendix. The formula of the *Act of Oblation*, likewise in the Appendix of the original work, has also been integrated in the text (at the end of the present chapter) for the same reason.

who burn with desire to satisfy His Justice by
taking on themselves the punishments due to
sinners. She had never heard of anyone, on the
other hand, who had deliberately offered to
make amends to God, by a formal act, for the
rejection of His love—that love which He
yearns to send coursing in torrents upon the
humble and simple ones of earth, and on those
" little souls " signed with the seal of Spiritual
Childhood; on all pious souls in fact, and even
on the vast multitudes of the indifferent and of
sinners.

This grieved Thérèse and, desiring to compassionate the good God, she was inspired to
offer herself as a victim to His love in order to
make reparation for man's rejection of that same
love. Then Almighty God would be free to
deluge the heart of His Thérèse with the ocean
of love stored up in His bosom.

Through her " Act of Oblation as *Victim of
Holocaust* to God's Merciful Love," Thérèse
begged God to let her soul be *drowned* in the
torrent of His Infinite Tenderness, " that " (in
this way) " I may become a *martyr* to thy love,
O my God ! "

Her choice of the word " victim " was perfect
for her intention. She thought of herself as a
tiny vessel, a " little thimble." [14]   Is it not an

---

[14] Cf. *Autobiography*, Chapter 2, page 52. " One day I expressed
surprise that God does not give an equal amount of glory to all

actual torment for the "thimble" to find the ocean bearing in upon it in a tidal wave of love? To be swept away completely, to be engulfed —what ineffable martyrdom !

We must not, however, confuse this with the martyrdom of victims of justice. Thérèse's heart was wounded, it is true, but here, love was answered by love, and as Ruysbroeck has written " . . . The wound of love ! indeed there is nothing that is sweeter, nor more terrible."

To be consumed by the Divine Tenderness was precisely what Thérèse had implored. Christ was not only a torrent; He was the Sun, " *searing* the victim with His rays." Saint Thérèse yearned to be " inundated," " to be burned up " by this love. She sought for more than she was capable of receiving, for she knew that in this way the Infinite Goodness and Mercy of God would overpower her. The new state of victim she proposed was *martyrdom* indeed, but a *martyrdom of love*.

Saint Thérèse dared to offer her Act of Oblation to her chosen " legion " of " little souls " because she did not identify the martyrdom of love with that call to suffering which distinguishes the victims of God's justice. To

the inhabitants of heaven. I was afraid they would not all be happy. You sent me to fetch Papa's big tumbler and putting it beside my tiny thimble, filled both with water, and asked me which seemed to be the fuller . . ."

help weak souls, Thérèse appeals to the *mercy* of the Heart of God, to His paternal condescension. She holds up before Him their very misery to invite His holy compassion. She calls on Him to regard their insignificance with pity, for she is convinced that " love to be fully satisfied must stoop even to nothingness."

It was His love, that love which she had made her own, which Thérèse yearned to contemplate in her God. She knew that God's love was fully *satisfied only when it had abased itself to nothingness* . . . " in order to transform that nothingness into fire." She believed herself to be too small to reach up to God, but that He in His Mercy would reach down and lift her up to Himself. Cradled in His Arms she would be transformed by His light, absolved of every fault, purified of every imperfection. " At every moment," she tells us, " this merciful love renews and purifies me, leaving in my soul no trace of sin." God cannot be satisfied she says, until He has raised to His Sacred Heart even the least of us; and there, like a runaway lamb, at the shepherd's bosom we may rest, held tenderly captive, victims of His divine love."

* * *

The sharp physical and moral sufferings of her last years on earth should be considered in conjunction with her call to ransom sinners in union with Jesus the Redeemer. This idea of ransom includes the assaults of the demon on souls like hers, overwhelmed with grace.

Saint Peter, Vicar of Our Lord Jesus Christ and Head of His Church on earth, declares that " the devil like a roaring lion goeth about seeking whom he may devour." This evil one who has a far keener perception of the spirit world than we, as creatures, could ever possibly have, certainly must have in some way sensed that an ocean of grace was being poured out on her who was to become the leader of countless souls in her future " legion."

Is it not possible, therefore, that just as in the case of the holy man, Job, Satan one day appeared before God and said: " It is not surprising that Thérèse loves you for she speaks to you, as it were, face to face. But withdraw from her and see if she will persevere in her confidence in you."

Almighty God was sure of His little spouse who was His pride and joy and, just as He had allowed His faithful servant Job to be tempted, so perhaps He permitted the evil one to wreak his malice this time on Thérèse. If this were so, it would be logical to assume that the enemy of mankind would carry out his design with violence reinforced by the bitter jealousy of one who will be loveless forever.

Had I probed into Thérèse's own attitude to her poignant interior trial of faith [15] and to her intolerable physical sufferings, I think I should have learned that she might have been *tempted*, if only for a moment, to wonder in anguish if the sufferings of the victims of love were not, after all, the same as those of the victims of God's justice. That one agonizing instant past, however, I would have heard her answer assuringly:

> "No, I could never have believed it possible to have suffered so much . . . never, never ! *I can only explain it by my intense desire to save souls.*"

The Saint's voluntary participation in the Passion of Christ (a participation foreseen, to be sure, in her Act of Oblation according to the degree willed by Our Lord) is the reason for her extraordinary sufferings, especially during those last years of her life.

The two burning ideals of Thérèse's vocation, therefore—ideals which, while not opposed, are situated on two different planes—might be expressed in this way:

1. From July 1887, when she was fourteen years old, she voiced the desire to suffer and to help save souls by the Cross. [16]

---

[15] For the space of eighteen months, Saint Thérèse had suffered grievous temptations against faith.

[16] Cf. *Autobiography*, p. 87. "One Sunday (in July 1887) on closing my book at the end of Mass, a picture of the Crucifixion slipped partly out, showing one of the Divine Hands pierced and

2. On June 9, 1895, the feast of the Most Holy Trinity, when, at the summit of her spiritual ascent, she offered herself as a victim to the merciful love of God; to make amends to this love which is on all sides ignored and rejected.

* * *

I heard my holy little sister affirm on her death-bed: "Fortunately I did not ask for suffering, for if I had prayed for it, then it would be my own suffering and I should fear not to have the strength to endure it." We must conclude from this that Thérèse was not identifying her *desires* of a life-time with a *formal petition* which should have bound her irrevocably. The distinction is inescapable. The soul offering herself to love is not asking for suffering, but in yielding herself up entirely to the designs of love, she is accepting in advance all that divine Providence will be pleased to send her by way of joys, labours and trials; at the same time, she counts on infinite mercy to enable her to sanctify her crosses by an enduring spirit of joy.

---

bleeding . . . I resolved to remain continuously at the foot of the Cross that I might receive the dew of salvation and pour it out on souls . . . I was consumed with an insatiable thirst for souls and I longed at any cost to snatch them from the everlasting flames of hell."

When the Liturgical Office of Saint Thérèse of the Child Jesus was given to the Church, the summarized ninth lesson of Matins contained these words: " . . . *inflamed with the desire of suffering*, she offered herself, two years before her death, as a victim to the merciful love of God." But Mère Agnès de Jésus (our sister) had no rest until she obtained, from the Sacred Congregation of Rites, a modification of this text. It was solely due to her intervention that, finally, on May 2, 1932, the substitute phrase was published in the *Acta Apostolicae Sedis* " . . . *on fire with divine love* . . . " which is a faithful expression of Thérèsian thought.

*   *   *

A new question arises here: what is the relation—if any—between Thérèse's *Act of Oblation* and the *Death of Love* described by Saint John of the Cross in the *Living Flame of Love?*

To my mind, Thérèse's understanding of the *Life of Love* and the *Death of Love* had its foundation in the doctrine of the Mystical Doctor of Carmel who, when treating of the *Life of Love*, writes: " It is of the highest importance that the soul exercise itself much in love so that its course may be quickly finished here below and that it may without delay see God face to face." [17]

—————————
[17] *Living Flame of Love*, p. 38.

Saint Thérèse, who realized that she was dying in her youth, consummated in love, quite naturally attached great importance to this counsel of her holy Father, Saint John.[18] In this connection, I should like to call attention to her poem, entitled *Vivre d'Amour*, in order to throw some light on one of the stanzas. This poem, which, in the original consisted of fourteen stanzas, was composed in its entirety during one of Thérèse's hours of Adoration before the Blessed Sacrament at " les Quarante-Heures "[19] in February 1895. It would not, therefore, be temerarious to believe that it was written under supernatural promptings and, as such, comprises the sum of the Saint's aspirations. In its first draft, the poem contained little or no reference to suffering, and as I was undergoing an acute trial at the time, Thérèse, at my request, wrote this new stanza to console me:

> " To live of love is not to fix one's tent
>   On Thabor's height and there with Thee
>   remain !
> It is to climb our Calvary with strength
>   nigh spent

---

[18] On her death-bed Saint Thérèse told Mère Agnès that from the beginning of her religious life, she constantly reminded herself of this counsel of Saint John of the Cross. Cf. *Novissima Verba*, p. 65.

[19] Forty Hours Adoration.

And count the heavy cross our truest
gain." [20]

On the other hand, the hymn, as Thérèse
composed it, does refer to the *sweetness of the
wound* of love and to its *delightful suffering*. But
then there is this other line:

" To die of love ! Oh ! martyrdom *most
sweet* ! " This proves also that in her concept of
the *Death of Love*, the Saint is one with Saint
John of the Cross who, when writing of the
" ineffable transports " of the soul at that supreme
moment, likens them to the *song of the dying
swan*. Faced with this and plunged as she was
in the last years of her life in an abyss of bitter
suffering of body and soul—even to the moment
of death—Thérèse could find refuge only in
these words of hers which we have quoted:

" *I can only explain it by my intense desire to save
souls* ! "

It was her *love of souls*, then, that she could
equate with her extraordinary sufferings, sufferings which aligned her with Our Lord in her
co-operative rôle in the mystery of Redemption.

And just as Jesus, in His mysterious dereliction
on the Cross, when He could no longer address

---

[20] The four remaining lines of this stanza (which Thérèse later
inserted between the third and fourth stanzas of her original
composition) read:
" Above my life a life of love shall be
The heavy cross shall then be gone for aye
Then here below in suffering with Thee,
Love ! let me stay ! "

God as His Father, cried out in mortal anguish: " My God ! My God ! why hast Thou forsaken me! ", so was it with Thérèse. Without ceasing to dwell in the depths of her soul, God, in a certain way, withdrew from her, and then allowed her all alone, so to speak, to taste all the bitterness of this piercing sorrow. " Souls are saved only by the Cross " we are told. Her heavenly Father, in allowing her to drain the chalice (which had become for her a mine of gold) thus fulfilled Thérèse's desire *to save souls*, a desire which was parallel with, and which was as often expressed as, her yearning to become a *victim of the love of God*.

But this latter desire would also be realized, and in the very way she had anticipated—nay, more magnificently realized ! After Thérèse " *had gone down into the valley of death* " [21] for the ransom of sinners, Almighty God manifested Himself to His faithful little spouse at the last instant of life in a *sublime ecstasy* whose *delightful assaults* " broke the web of the sweet encounter ! " [22] And in that long-desired *Death of Love* about which she had sung in faith during her brief exile in this world, the sweet victim gently expired. [23]

---

[21] Ps. XXII.

[22] *Living Flame of Love*, p. 34.

[23] " Break the web of the sweet encounter ! " . . . " I have always applied these words (of Saint John of the Cross) to the

It was during Mass on Trinity Sunday, June 9, 1895, that Saint Thérèse was strongly inspired to make this *Act of Oblation to God's Merciful Love*.

I noticed, on leaving the choir after Mass that morning, that she was visibly moved. Then when she made a sign for me to come after her, I was somewhat puzzled until I realized that we were following Mère Agnès de Jésus, our Prioress, who was on her way to the Turn. We soon caught up with Reverend Mother, and as Thérèse, in a few inarticulate words,[24] began to make known her request, she became a little embarrassed. She was asking permission to offer herself, with me, to the merciful love of God, although I do not remember whether she actually pronounced the word " victim." As the matter seemed unimportant, Mère Agnès consented without further inquiry. When the two of us were alone again, I saw that Thérèse's face had become as though transfigured, and in a few words, she went on to explain her plan to me: she would gather her thoughts together on paper and then compose an *Act of Self-Oblation*. Two days later, on June 11th, we knelt together before the shrine of *The Miraculous Virgin of the Smile* which was in the art-room adjoining my little sister's cell. It was there before Our

---

death of love which I desire. Love will not wear out the web of my life, it will break it suddenly." The Saint's words to Mère Agnès. Cf. *Novissima Verba*, p. 65.

[24] " Elle balbutia quelques mots . . . "

Blessed Mother that Thérèse recited the Act of Oblation for both of us. Later on, the Saint communicated her secret to another novice, Soeur Marie de La Trinité, and also to our eldest sister, Marie du Sacré Coeur.

Then she wrote about it in her autobiography, and invited *all little souls* to share her riches. According to the Saint, this offering is not the equivalent of asking for an avalanche of supererogatory sufferings; it is, rather, a question of abandoning self, with unparalleled confidence to God's Infinite Mercy. Our eldest sister, Marie du Sacré Coeur, refused at first to make this Act of Oblation, for she had no desire, she said, for any additional trials. In this connection, Soeur Marie's infirmarian in later years recorded the following story in her diary:

"Today, June 6, 1934, I was speaking with Soeur Marie du Sacré Coeur about the *Act of Oblation to Merciful Love.* She told me that she was raking the grass in the quadrangle one day in 1895 when Soeur Thérèse who was close by, asked if she would like to offer herself as a victim to the *merciful love of God.* 'Indeed not,' Soeur Marie replied at once, 'for if I offered myself as victim, God would take me at my word, and I have a great dread of suffering. Besides, far from inspiring me, the word *victim* has always repelled me.'

"Then *Little Thérèse* told her that she could well understand how she felt, but that to offer

ourselves as victims to the *Love of God* is entirely
different from giving ourselves over to His
justice. It does not necessarily mean, she explained, an increase of suffering but merely the
ability to love the good God more, and to make
up for those souls who do not want to love Him.
Thérèse's eloquence finally convinced her sister.
' She won me over to her idea,' Soeur Marie
said, ' and I have never regretted having taken
the step.' "

Here I might add that in subsequent years
when, as eldest sister and godmother of Saint
Thérèse, Marie found herself dedicated to an
extended circle of friends and benefactors to
Carmel, she proved to be one of the most ardent
apostles of *the Act of Oblation*. She never hesitated
to propose this *Offering* to her numerous
correspondents, and, over that long period of
years, she met with only one refusal, as far as I
know. And it was while renewing this *Oblation*,
in muffled tones, it is true, but distinctly
articulating the words, that Soeur Marie du
Sacré Coeur gave up her pure soul to God on
January 19, 1940, at two-thirty in the morning.
It will be interesting now to read the account
of one of my companions in the novitiate, Soeur
Marie de La Trinité:

"It was not until November 30, 1895, that
Soeur Thérèse spoke to me for the first time of
her *Act of Oblation* to the merciful love of God.

At once I expressed an ardent desire to make this *Offering* myself, and we decided that I should do so the next day. But a more serious consideration of the matter in the solitude of our cell convinced me that an act of such importance called for a longer and more prayerful preparation. When I gave Soeur Thérèse my reason for desiring to delay, her face lit up and she answered: ' Oh yes ! this act is far more important than we could imagine; but would you know the only preparation that God requires? It is a humble and sincere recognition of our unworthiness, and since that grace has already been granted to you, offer yourself to Him freely and without any fear. Tomorrow, then, following our Thanksgiving after Holy Communion, you shall make this Offering with me. We shall kneel together in the Oratory before the Blessed Sacrament exposed, and while you are reciting the *Act of Oblation*, I shall offer you to Jesus as the little victim whom I have prepared for Him.' "

Here we have an additional proof that if our Saint believed that this *Offering to Merciful Love* would necessarily bring a torrent of suffering in its train, she would not have allowed us to act so precipitately in the matter. On the other hand, she always insisted that " from this *Oblation* of self to God's love, we can expect *mercy* alone. We have nothing to fear from this Act," she often exclaimed with holy ardour.

She was careful to point out at all times,

nevertheless, that good will and a spirit of generosity play leading parts in this dedication to *Merciful Love*. " Good will and generosity," the Saint frequently repeated; and we might add that these essential dispositions are fortified *by the grace of the sacrament of the present moment.* The *Act of Oblation* intensifies this grace to a marvellous degree, and the divine assistance is as instantaneous and efficacious as the gift of self is spontaneous and complete.

* * *

THE FORMULA OF SAINT THÉRÈSE'S ACT OF OBLATION

Act of Oblation of myself as Victim of Holocaust to the Merciful Love of the Good God.[25]

O My God, Most Blessed Trinity, I desire to love Thee and to make Thee loved, to labour for the glorification of Holy Church by saving souls on earth and by delivering those who suffer in Purgatory. I desire to accomplish Thy will perfectly and to attain to the degree of glory which Thou hast prepared for me in Thy Kingdom; in a word, I long to be a saint; but I know that I am powerless, and I implore Thee, O my God, to be Thyself my sanctity.

[25] Saint Thérèse carried this Act of Oblation in a copy of the Holy Gospels near to her heart night and day. This copy of the Act of Oblation is from the *original* of Saint Thérèse's Act.

Since Thou hast so loved me as to give me Thine only Son to be my Saviour and my Spouse, the infinite treasures of His merits are mine; to Thee I offer them with joy, beseeching Thee to behold me only through the Face of Jesus and in His Heart burning with *love*.

Again, I offer Thee all the merits of the saints (in heaven and on earth), their acts of love and those of the holy angels; and finally I offer Thee, O Blessed Trinity, the love and the merits of the Holy Virgin, my most dear Mother; to her I entrust my oblation, begging her to present it to Thee.

Her Divine Son, my well-beloved Spouse, during the days of His life on earth told us: "If you ask the Father anything in My name, He will give it to you." [26] I am then certain that Thou wilt hearken to my desires. Yes, my God, I am sure of this: the more Thou willest to give, the more dost Thou make us desire.

Immense are the desires that I feel within my heart, and with confidence I call upon Thee to come and take possession of my soul. Ah! I cannot receive Thee in Holy Communion as often as I would; but, Lord, art Thou not Almighty? . . . Remain in me as in the Tabernacle; never leave Thy little victim . . .

I long to console Thee for the ingratitude of the wicked, and I pray Thee to take from me the

---

[26] John XVI, 23.

power to displease Thee. If through frailty sometimes I fall, may Thy divine glance purify my soul immediately, consuming every imperfection, like fire which transforms all things into itself . . .

I thank Thee, O my God, for all the graces Thou hast showered upon me, in particular for having made me pass through the crucible of suffering. It is with joy that I shall behold Thee on the last day bearing Thy sceptre, the Cross; since Thou has deigned to give me for my portion this most precious cross, I have hope of resembling Thee in heaven, and of seeing the sacred stigmata of Thy passion shine in my glorified body . . .

After the exile on earth, I hope to enjoy the possession of Thee in *La Patrie*, but I have no wish to amass merits for heaven; I will work for Thy love alone, my sole aim being to give Thee pleasure, to console Thy Sacred Heart, and to save souls who will love Thee forever.

At the evening of this life I shall appear before Thee with empty hands, for I ask not, Lord, that Thou wouldst count my works. All our justices are tarnished in Thy sight; therefore I desire to be clothed with Thine own justice, and to receive from Thy love the eternal possession of Thyself. I crave no other throne, no other crown but Thee, O my Well-Beloved . . .

In Thy sight time is nothing; one day is as

a thousand years.[27]   Thou canst in an instant prepare me to appear before Thee . . .

That my life may be one act of perfect love, I offer myself as Victim of Holocaust to Thy Merciful Love, imploring Thee to consume me unceasingly, and to let the flood-tide of infinite tenderness, pent up in Thee, overflow into my soul, that so I may become a very martyr of Thy love, O my God.

May this martyrdom, having first prepared me to appear before Thee, break life's thread at last, and may my soul take its flight unhindered to the eternal embrace of Thy Merciful love . . .

I desire, O my Well-Beloved, at every heart-beat, to renew this oblation an infinite number of times, till the shadows have disappeared,[28] and I can tell Thee my love eternally face to face . . .

(Signed) MARIE-FRANÇOISE-THÉRÈSE DE L'ENFANT JÉSUS ET DE LA SAINTE FACE,

Rel. Carm. Ind.

Feast of the Most Holy Trinity,
Sunday, June 9, 1895.

---

[27] Cf. Ps. LXXXIX, 4.
[28] Cf. Cant. IV, 6.

CHAPTER IV

UNION WITH GOD

" IT is the spirit of gratitude which draws down upon us the overflow of God's grace," our Mistress said to me one day, " for no sooner have we thanked Him for one blessing than He hastens to send us ten additional favours in return. Then, when we show our gratitude for these new gifts, He multiplies His benedictions to such a degree that there seems to be a constant stream of divine grace ever coming our way." She added, " This has been my own personal experience; try it out for yourself and see. For all that Our Lord is constantly giving me, my gratitude is boundless, and I try to prove it to Him in a thousand different ways."

Even in her human contacts, Thérèse was always outstanding for this virtue of gratitude, however trifling the favour might be. There was an added dimension to her spirit of gratitude, however, with regard to those priests who, in Our Lord's place, had, from time to time, solved her spiritual difficulties; to these bene-factors she was eternally grateful.

One day, when I was lamenting the fact that God seemed to have abandoned me completely, Thérèse energetically admonished me:

> " Oh ! don't speak like that ! You know well that at times I, too, become perplexed about circumstances or the turn of events, but I try to keep on smiling; I even turn to Our Lord and say ' Thank You.' We are disloyal to His Love whenever we do not trust Him completely. Please ! never any ' imprecations ' against divine Providence, but only, and always, a spirit of deep and lasting gratitude ! "

* * *

I was under an illusion that in entering Carmel I was doing something grand and heroic for Jesus. I asked my Little Thérèse, therefore, to write some verses, to the air " Rappelle-toi," which should remind Our Lord of all that I was sacrificing for Him and of all that our family had suffered for His love. The Saint received my petition with evident pleasure because, as I was soon to realize, she intended by this means to bring home a salutary lesson to me. Consequently, when later I pored over the innumerable couplets of her beautiful poem " Remember Thou," I could find no reference whatever to any sacrifice I might have made for Jesus; each verse was, on the contrary, a telling reminder of all that He had done for me !

I could not help thinking of the Gospel parable of the Pharisee and the Publican. Had I not, like the proud Pharisee, boasted that I have given tithes of all I possessed ? This incident also brought home to me the truth that there was no stopping Thérèse in her determination to make me forget self entirely, in order that I might inhale the pure air of love and thanksgiving.

* * *

The thought that there were some religious communities who were submitting to unjust laws against the Church promulgated by the anti-Catholic secular power, filled me with indignation. One day in Thérèse's presence I exclaimed, " My entire being rises up in rebellion when I witness such a spirit of cowardice. I would be cut into a thousand pieces rather than belong to any of these communities or to assist them in any way." The Saint answered:

" We should not be concerned about such matters at all. It is true that I would be of your opinion and act perhaps in the same way had I any responsibility in the matter. But I have no obligation whatsoever. Moreover, *our only duty is to become united to God*. Even if we were members of those communities which are being

publicly criticized for their defections, we would
be greatly at fault in becoming disquieted on
that account."

* * *

Thérèse was ever on the alert to stem the
current of my natural impetuosity which was
always in focus in my external activity. I was
far too eager about my assignments, and I seemed
to be pushed by an irresistible drive to carry
them out, meticulously, to an exaggerated stage
of perfection. Consequently, whenever I did
not achieve this, I experienced a sense of
frustration. Then Thérèse would tell me:

> "You have not come to Carmel merely to
> turn out a mountain of work or even, strictly
> speaking, to become an *indefatigable* worker.
> Are you unduly concerned at the present
> moment as to what is happening in other
> Carmelite Monasteries, and whether the nuns
> there are busy or not? Does their work interfere
> with your prayer and meditation? Well, in the
> same way you should become detached from
> your daily occupations, conscientiously devoting
> to them the time prescribed but with perfect
> freedom of heart. ' I remember reading,' she
> continued, ' that when the Israelites were
> building the walls of Jerusalem, each labourer
> while working held a sword in one hand.'¹ That

---

¹ Esdras II, 4, 11.

is a symbol of the interior attitude we should acquire in the matter of work: that at the point of the sword, we hold off all dissipation of soul in our external labours."

Nevertheless, Thérèse was always careful not to stress this point of utter disinterestedness in the case of those souls who needed a push in the opposite direction, for she could not endure any careless or negligent approach to duty. She knew, as we all know, that, in this matter of physical exertion especially, there are those, in religion as in the world, who mistake a casual attitude for the virtue of holy indifference. Therefore, she continually urged us to give ourselves, heart and soul, to our appointed duties but to remain in the presence of God while doing so. She was always careful to point out, however, that any negligent performance of our tasks can be just as detrimental to the sacred presence of God as any over-eagerness; both extremes were to be shunned.

" When we are in love," Thérèse often told us, " even our external employments bear the marks of this love and we put great fervour into all our actions. The author of the *Imitation* said it for us all when he wrote, ' . . . the lover runneth and flieth . . . the lover findeth nothing impossible . . . for he cannot be restrained.' " [2]

---

[2] *Imit.*, Book III, Chap. 5.

Thérèse's whole bearing in choir was one of great modesty and recollection. In this she was an inspiration to us all. I asked her one day about her interior dispositions while reciting the Divine Office in choir and she replied that she had no fixed method of prayer at that time. She went on to say that often she transported herself in spirit, during the Office, to some desert-cliff high above this earth. There alone with Jesus, with the world at her feet, she would forget that creatures existed, and would simply tell Him over and over again how much she loved Him. True, she did not always understand the language she was using to express her love, but she added, it was enough for her to realize that she was making Him happy.[3]

She was always delighted when it was her turn to be hebdomadary [4] at the Office, for then like the priest at Mass she was privileged to read aloud the prayer of the day. On her death bed, she bore witness to her love and reverence for the Office in these words, " I do not believe that anyone could possibly desire more than I to recite the Divine Office perfectly and without a mistake."

---

[3] Thérèse did not read Latin; consequently she could not dwell on the literal meaning of the text of the Divine Office. During the actual recitation, however, she was always quick to grasp the meaning of certain passages which she had previously read in French translation.

[4] The religious designated to have the chief rôle in the Divine Office.

She told me that after she had asked *the inhabitants of heaven to adopt her as their child*, she used to listen each morning with special reverence and devotion to the Martyrology at Prime when the " roll-call " of her " close relatives up there " was read aloud in choir.[5]

* * *

Thérèse did not want us to pass on to another Sister any amusing or distracting thought just before we went to chant the Divine Office. In this way, we should avoid many unnecessary distractions, she told us, and the thought could always be communicated later. She was extremely vigilant in this matter herself and faithfully adhered to this counsel at all times.

* * *

The Saint lived out the span of her entire life in pure faith, accepting the dark night of her spirit uncomplainingly. I do not believe that a soul ever received less consolation in prayer. Her annual retreats and monthly recollection days were times of great spiritual deprivation. For seven years of her religious life, she was plunged in great aridity; she told me this privately at the end of her life.

---

[5] Here Saint Thérèse is referring to the commemoration of the saints of the day which is read aloud at Prime.

This lack of tangible consolation, nevertheless, made her only more assiduous during the time of formal prayer and meditation. She was happy, she said, to be able, on account of her aridity, to give God more in those hours. Thérèse was firm in the conviction that not even a moment should be taken from the time assigned to mental prayer, and she trained the novices accordingly.

One day when we had to remain in the laundry after the bell for prayer, she noticed my eagerness about the work. " What are you doing ? " she asked. " I am busy with the wash, of course! " I answered promptly. " That's all very well," she enjoined, " but interiorly you should be striving to make your prayer. This is God's time and it should not be stolen from Him."

* * *

Her own interior union with God was as simple and natural as her conversations with Him. When I asked one day how often she forgot the presence of God, she answered quite simply, " I do not believe I have ever been more than three minutes at a time without thinking of Him."

Such close application seemed hardly possible to me and I told her so. She replied, " Isn't it true that we naturally think of someone whom we dearly love ? "

For her hours of meditation, Thérèse leaned heavily on the Gospels and, in a lesser degree, on certain books of the Old Testament.[6] This was especially true of the latter part of her life when no other book, even among those books which had helped her in previous years, succeeded in enkindling her devotion.

Incidentally, one of the books from which she had drawn great profit was Bossuet's Essay, *La Vie Cachée en Dieu*. As soon as I had entered Carmel, she suggested that I read it.

At the beginning of her religious life, Thérèse asked me (I was still at home) to procure Monsignor de Segur's work entitled *Grandeurs en Jésus*. This book describes the glory which our souls may attain through Jesus. But if the Saint ever consented to consider her grandeur in Christ this was only to recognize in Him her "littleness," in order to plumb its depths. According to her own expression, she preferred lights on her nothingness to lights on faith.

At that period of her life and also later on, she was fascinated by the works of Saint John of the Cross. When I came to the Monastery I witnessed her glowing enthusiasm when, as we examined together our Holy Father's *Map of Perfection*, we came to the line: " Here there is no longer any way because there is no law for the just man."

---

[6] At that period, young religious were not always permitted to read all the books of the Old Testament.

My little Thérèse then became breathless with emotion as she tried to express her happiness. Her daring confidence in the mercy of God had been interpreted as a kind of presumption by some members of the community, but this assurance on the part of Saint John of the Cross seemed to give wings to her independent explorations in the ways of divine love.

In her desire to attain to the spiritual summits, she was in this way emboldened to trace out a new way, *The Way of Spiritual Childhood*. No longer, however, can it, strictly speaking, be called a way because by its swift and direct current we are raised like a rocket to the very Heart of God Himself.

I am strongly convinced that Thérèse's entire life of prayer was continually converging towards a deeper experimental knowledge of "this science of love."

* * *

HER SPIRITUAL LIFE

The Saint was highly gifted with profound understanding of divine things, and she possessed a very clear knowledge of the principles of the spiritual life. Her excellent memory enabled her always to recall the best of whatever she had read or heard. In this way she found it easy to illustrate a point by a little anecdote or by some other shrewd observation.

This was true especially in the field of Holy Scripture. At Carmel the Bible was her greatest treasure, and it was with amazing ease and keen perception that she was able to assimilate various passages of Holy Writ; she found no difficulty in discovering their hidden meaning and then in applying the lesson in a very unusual way. I had made a copy [7] of several books of the Old Testament, and I gave it to her. This proved to be her invaluable aid in her hours of prayer.

In order to know God and to learn more about *His Character*, she studied the sacred writings and in particular the holy Gospels. The differences in the translations of Scripture deeply distressed her.

" If I had been a priest," she told me, " I would have studied Greek and Hebrew in order to

---

[7] After Thérèse's entrance to Carmel, her sister Céline, while still in the world, began to copy these passages, first from her uncle's (Monsieur Guérin) large, expensive Bible (Bourasse et Janvier edition) and then, for practical reasons, from a smaller copy of less value. (Translation by Lemaistre de Sacy, 1864). Soeur Geneviève's manuscript comprises the following books of the Old Testament in the order in which they appear in her copy-book:

> Canticle of Canticles, Ecclesiastes, Wisdom, Proverbs, Isaias, Tobias, Ecclesiasticus, Ezechiel, Osee, Habacuc, Sophonias, Malachias, Joel, Amos, Micheas, Zacharias.

When Soeur Geneviève entered Carmel on September 14, 1894, she gave this manuscript copy to Thérèse, who used it thereafter for her mediation and spiritual reading. In all likelihood, it was in this little book that she had read the sentence which proved to be the theme-song of her life: " Whosoever is a little one, let him come to Me." (*Proverbs*, IX, 4. Also quoted in the *Autobiography*, Chapter IX).

understand the divine word of God as He deigned to express it in our human language." [8]

Day and night she carried the book of the Gospels next to her heart. To procure a like happiness for us, her novices, she was constantly looking around for single copies of each of the four Gospels; these fastened together were more easily worn over the heart than a cumbersome volume of all four texts combined.

* * *

Saint Thérèse of the Child Jesus had great devotion to the Most Holy Trinity, and she

---

[8] It is interesting to learn how Thérèse, without any complete copies of the Old Testament at her disposal, could have noticed the divergence in the various translations of the Bible. We are told that the Saint compared Soeur Geneviève's small manuscript copy with the different translations of the *Psalter* of the Divine Office (principally the *Glair* edition) and with the *Prophetical Books*. Her *Manuel de Chretien* contained: *The New Testament, the Psalms, The Imitation of Christ,* the *Ordinary of the Mass* (with its numerous texts from Scripture), *Vespers,* and *Compline* (Edited by Mame et Fils, Tours, 1864). This text of the Psalms had been translated from the Hebrew—with the approval of the Archbishop of Tours, although the translator's name was not given.

There were other works with long extracts from the Bible to which Soeur Thérèse had access such as: the French translation of the *Breviary* (the translation of the Divine Office is read in the vernacular each day in the Carmelite refectory); the Latin-French *Holy Week Ceremonial; Les Paroissiens;* Dom Gueranger's *Liturgical Year; The Works of Saint John of the Cross,* and others.

Her frequent quotations from the Sacred Writings prove that Saint Thérèse had drawn from all these sources.

(Translator's note. It is well to remember this when reading Saint Thérèse in view of the fact that the sources of her scriptural quotations can be indicated, in most cases, by a reference only).

ardently desired that this feast be raised to a higher rank in the calendar of the Church. Before I joined her at the Monastery, she used to call me first " Marie de La Trinité " and then later on, " Marie de la Sainte Face." This second name was officially given to me when I entered Carmel. But some months later my name was changed to Soeur Geneviève in memory of Mère Geneviève, the saintly foundress of our Carmel. Meanwhile, another novice had been given the title " de La Trinité," and this made Thérèse very happy.

It was during Mass on the feast of the Most Holy Trinity that Thérèse was inspired to offer herself up as a *Victim of Holocaust to God's Merciful Love.*

* * *

On entering Thérèse's cell one day, I was struck by her heavenly expression of recollection. Although she was sewing industriously, she seemed to be lost in profound contemplation. When I inquired, " What are you thinking about ? " she replied with tears in her eyes: " I am meditating on the *Our Father*. It is so sweet to call God our Father ! "

* * *

She loved God as a child loves his father with outbursts of incredible tenderness. One day during her illness, when referring to Him, she said " Papa " when she had meant to say " God." It seemed to her that we were smiling over her slip, and with much feeling she told us: " Nevertheless, He is indeed my ' Papa,' and it is a consolation for my heart to be able to call Him by that name ! "

* * *

Jesus was, in truth, the supreme love of her heart. In a spirit of great reverence she always capitalized the first letter of the pronouns which refer to His Adorable Person.

One day she asked me: " When you are praying, do you like to address Jesus with the familiar *Tu* or the formal *Vous?* " I replied that I prefer to use *Tu*.

Much consoled, she went on, " I like to say *Tu* also, because that more truly expresses the intimate love I have for Him. I always address Him in this way in my conversations with Him, but I do not dare to do so in my poems and prayers when they are to be read by others." [9]

---

[9] In the French tradition, particularly at that period, this distinction was made much of. We are told that Thérèse's father had always used the formal *Vous* when addressing his parents. It was only with reluctance that he agreed to Madame Martin's request to allow Thérèse and her sisters to use the familiar *Tu* with their parents.

Devotion to the Holy Face was, for Thérèse, the crown and complement of her love for the Sacred Humanity of Our Lord. This Blessed Face was the mirror wherein she beheld the *Heart* and the *Soul* of her Well-Beloved. Just as the picture of a loved one serves to bring the whole person before us, so in the Holy Face of Christ, Thérèse beheld the *entire Humanity* of Jesus. We can say unequivocally that this devotion was the burning inspiration of the Saint's life.

Furthermore, in our appraisal of her devotional life at Carmel, we must recognize, in the interests of objective truth, that her devotion to the Holy Face of Jesus transcended—or more accurately embraced—all the other attractions of her spiritual life.

It was from the contemplation of the agonizing Face of Jesus that Thérèse drew strength for all those courageous acts of exalted virtue which characterized her life: it was in the meditation of the humiliated Face of Jesus that she learned to exercise herself in humility and detachment from creatures, in love of suffering and in generous self-sacrifice; this love was the motive force of her zeal for the salvation of souls.

In this she was, without being aware of it, only exemplifying Our Lord's words to Saint Gertrude when He told her: " Let the soul who is desirous of advancing in perfection hasten with great alacrity to My Sacred Heart. But he who yearns to make even greater progress and to *mount still higher* on the wings of desire must rise with the swiftness of an eagle and *hover about* My Sacred Face, supported like a seraph on the wings of a magnanimous love."

Thérèse did just that. The consequence of her flight was a truly seraphic love yielding fruits a hundredfold of heroic generosity. It was the Face of Jesus which she pointed out to her novices, as the book wherein she had learned the science of love and the art of practising all the virtues.

All her writings—the *Autobiography*, the *Letters* and the *Poems*—are impregnated with love of this same Adorable Face. She inscribed this motto close to the picture of the Holy Face on her coat-of-arms: " Love is repaid by love alone."

In the year 1904, seven years after her death, I succeeded in reproducing my first copy of the Holy Face of the Winding Sheet of Turin; this, I am sure, was due to her intercession before the throne of God in heaven. I have always believed, moreover, that it was through her merits while still on earth that I was inspired, in the first place, to study the Holy Shroud with a view to a reproduction of the Divine Features on canvas.

This is a copy of her *Act of Consecration to the Holy Face* which was written for the Novitiate: [10]

---

[10] In a recent edition of *Histoire d'une Ame* (1953) we read that the Saint wrote this prayer for her own devotion and also for Soeur

" O Adorable Face of Jesus ! since Thou hast been pleased to make special choice of our souls in order to give Thyself to them, we come to consecrate ourselves to Thee.

" We seem to hear, O Jesus, Thy invitation: ' Open to me, My sisters, My beloved spouses, for My face is wet with the dew, and my locks with the drops of the night.' [11]   Our souls understand Thy language of love; we desire to wipe Thy sweet Face, and to console Thee for the forgetfulness of the wicked. In their eyes Thou art still, as it were, hidden . . . they esteem Thee an object of reproach !

" O Blessed Face ! more lovely than the lilies and roses of springtime ! Thou art not hidden from us. The tears which veil from us Thy *Divine Gaze* are as precious diamonds which we delight to treasure up, and through their infinite value, to purchase the souls of our brethren.

" From Thine adorable lips we have heard Thy loving plaint, ' I thirst.' We know that the thirst which consumes Thee is the thirst of

Geneviève and Soeur Marie de La Trinité, her two senior novices. The three signatures are affixed to the prayer:

Th. de L'Enfant Jésus et de La Sainte Face.
G. de Ste. Th., Marie de La Sainte Face.
M. de La Trinité de La Sainte Face.

This *Act of Consecration to the Holy Face* which is taken from the original autograph, is placed in an appendix in Soeur Geneviève's *Conseils et Souvenirs*.

[11] Cant. V, 2.

love, and in order to quench it we would desire to possess an infinite love !

" O Well-Beloved Spouse of our souls ! if we could have the love of all hearts, that love would be Thine . . .   Grant it to us, O Lord, and then come to Thy little spouses and quench Thy thirst . . .

" Souls, O God, give us souls ! We thirst for souls, for souls of apostles and martyrs above all, that through them, we may inflame all poor sinners with Thy love.

" O Adorable Face ! we shall win this grace from Thee ! Forgetting our exile, ' on the banks of the rivers of Babylon,' we shall sing in Thine ears the sweetest of melodies. And since Thou art the one, true home of our souls, our songs shall not be sung in a strange land.

" O Beloved Face of Jesus ! while awaiting the eternal day when we shall gaze upon Thine infinite glory, our only desire is to delight Thy divine Eyes by keeping *our faces* hidden, so that no one on earth may recognize us . . . Dear Jesus ! Heaven for us is Thy hidden countenance ! . . . "

* * *

It was the Holy Sacrifice of the Mass and the Sacrament of the Holy Eucharist which made Thérèse's entire life one of deep and abiding joy. She never undertook a matter of any importance without asking that a Mass might be offered for the intention. Whenever our aunt sent donations to Carmel for Thérèse's feast-days and other anniversaries, my little sister always asked permission to have these gifts converted into Mass-offerings. Sometimes she would whisper to me on those occasions, " The Masses are for my naughty child (Pranzini);[12] I must continue to assist him, you know ! "

When disposing of her temporal possessions before pronouncing the vow of poverty at profession Thérèse stipulated that the sum of money (100 francs) which she had left in her purse be used for Masses for our saintly father who was so ill at the time. She was supremely convinced that the Blood of Jesus, as it was lifted up in sacrifice on the altar, was the best guarantee of heaven's choicest graces for her loved one.

* * *

Daily Communion was not a current practice in the life of the Church in Thérèse's time; even in religious houses the privilege was rare and it was often conditioned by arbitrary regulations on the part of the immediate superiors. The privation proved to be one of my little sister's

---

[12] See note p. 147.

greatest sufferings in Carmel, and she began to pray that there might be a liberalizing change in this traditional legislation. In the year 1890, a decree of the Sovereign Pontiff, Leo XIII, allowing greater freedom for religious [13] on this point came, Thérèse believed, in answer to her prayers to Saint Joseph to whom she had confided this petition. Thereafter, whenever she passed his statue in the garden, she lovingly scattered flowers before him as a tribute of gratitude. The Saint predicted, while still living, that it would not be long after her death before we, at Carmel, should enjoy the privilege of daily Communion, and this prophecy was verified to the letter.[14]

Thérèse fulfilled the duties of Sacristan with loving eagerness; no task could have been more

---

[13] This decree of Leo XIII was dated December 17, 1890 and the following is the passage in question: " Our Most Holy Father has decreed that the ordinary confessor of religious communities shall henceforth enjoy exclusive powers concerning either the permission or the prohibition to approach the Holy Table. Superiors of religious are no longer free to interfere in any way in this legislation.   Those who have obtained the confessor's permission to receive Holy Communion more frequently, or even daily, are bound, however, to inform their Superiors of this authorization."   Actually, the confessor of Carmel, Abbé Youf, was not influenced by this decree to change the custom prevailing at the Carmel of Lisieux except when he allowed Thérèse to receive Communion daily, during the influenza epidemic, December 1891—January 1892.

[14] Abbé Youf died a few days after the Saint.   His successor, Abbé Hodierne, empowered by the Holy Father's decree, immediately introduced the practice of daily Communion at the Carmel of Lisieux.

in harmony with her ardent love for Christ in the Blessed Sacrament. Whenever, in the discharge of this office, she discovered a tiny particle of the Sacred Host which, through an oversight, had been left on the paten or on the corporal, her heart thrilled with joy. On one occasion when the ciborium had not been sufficiently purified, Thérèse called several of the novices to accompany her as she carried it with loving reverence and indescribable happiness to its proper place. Another time she became breathless with delight when at the Communion window she was able to hold up her scapular in time to receive the Sacred Host which had accidentally slipped through the fingers of the priest.

Before placing the particles destined to become the Body of Christ in the ciborium, she loved to see her own reflection at the bottom of the golden vessel where the Holy of Holies was soon to repose.

The fresco around our Oratory Tabernacle, a task which the Saint accomplished with much love and devotion, is a monument to her spirit of obedience; she was unfamiliar with the rudiments of artistic decorating and designing, and furthermore, there was no way of providing sufficient light for the work in that part of the Oratory. She was obliged, besides, to make use of a ladder while painting; even an experienced

artist should have been hindered in his work by
such handicaps. Thérèse, however, triumphed
over the difficulties and produced a very credit-
able piece of work. The little angels which
encircle the design are particularly attractive
with their expressions of heavenly beauty and
childlike innocence.

* * *

My sister's deep spirit of faith inspired her
with great reverence for priests because of their
sacerdotal dignity, a dignity which could never
be too highly esteemed. She often expressed a
certain regret at her own exclusion from the
priesthood, and in June 1897 when she knew
her illness was fatal, she naïvely said to me one
day,

> " The good God is taking me to heaven *before*
> the age when ordination usually takes place;
> He must want to spare me the chagrin of
> witnessing the actual frustration of my ardent
> desire to be a priest."

It made her very happy to learn that Saint
Barbara had brought the Blessed Sacrament
miraculously to Saint Stanislaus Kotska. " Why
was it a simple maiden," she asked, " and not
rather an angel or a priest ? Ah ! what marvels
shall we not behold in heaven ! I truly believe

that those who have so lovingly desired the priesthood and have not attained to it in this world will enjoy all its privileges in the next."

* * *

Thérèse had charge of the cloister-shrine of the Child Jesus and she used to give up part of her noon-rest hour in summer in order to decorate the little grotto. She had done it up in rose-colour and had it surrounded always with a bright array of wild-flowers and life-like little birds of iridescent plumage.[15]

Up to the time of Thérèse's entrance there had never been an abundance of flowers in our Carmel, and this proved to be no small privation for a little girl of fifteen, who had always found her delight in romping through country fields and meadows. To be able no longer to pick even a golden buttercup was part of Thérèse's holocaust. But Jesus was looking on, and once again He magnificently rewarded His little spouse, as she tells us in the following story:

> " During my first summer in Carmel, I began to wonder if ever again I would set eyes on my favourite poppies, on the little cornflowers and the marguerites; had the wonderful wheat-fields and the sheaves of grain disappeared forever? "

---

[15] " les petits oiseaux empailles "—little stuffed birds.

She was really beginning to experience a kind of nostalgia when, one day, our Sister-Portress brought in to Reverend Mother a large shock of the very wheat and wildflowers which Thérèse was longing to see again.   This rustic sheaf had been found on the extern-Sister's window casement; it was never discovered who had left it there.   And then, totally unaware of the desire she had been cherishing, our Mother handed over the gift to her for her Holy Child Shrine.

From that time on, our Carmel has always had an abundance of field-flowers.

The Saint found great devotion in gently tossing up her flowers to the large *Christus* in our quadrangle.   Often during her last illness, she could be seen lovingly covering her profession crucifix [16] with roses while carefully removing the withered petals.   One day I found her touching with her finger-tips the nails and the crown of thorns of her Jesus.   When I asked what she was doing, she answered—in a tone of mild embarrassment that I had noticed her, " I am removing His nails, and lifting the crown of thorns from His Brow ! "

On another occasion, when I placed some roses in her hand and asked her to toss them over to another nun as a sign of affection, she declined; she did not believe that creatures should be favoured with that particular tribute of love and devotion.

---

[16] Worn under the Scapular after profession.

Our Lady's statue—*La Vierge du Sourire*—
which had miraculously cured her mysterious
illness in childhood, was a source of much consolation to Thérèse at all times. This heavy
statue,[17] a family treasure, was moved to our
monastery when I entered Carmel, and Soeur
Thérèse was at the enclosure door to receive it.
To the surprise (and inspiration) of the nuns who
were with her, she caught up the statue in her
arms in a trice as though it were a feather, and
after lovingly caressing it, carried it off to its
destined shrine.

From then on, the Saint could be seen at
frequent intervals kneeling before this shrine,
and praying to Our Lady with glowing fervour.
During her last illness, Thérèse was unceasingly
turning her gaze towards this miraculous image,
which had been brought down to the Infirmary
and placed on a table facing her bed.

* * *

The Saint was always on the alert in distribut-
ing medals of Our Lady, and she had strong
faith in their power. While still in the world,
she tutored two little girls who were in need,
and each of them wore on their breast Our
Lady's medal fastened there by Thérèse herself.
She also succeeded in persuading an unbelieving
charwoman to wear one of these medals.

---

[17] It is a statue of very heavy plaster, thirty-six inches high.

One of her resolutions at the time of her First Communion was " to say the *Memorare* every day," a promise to which she was faithful to the end of her life. Later on, she also took up the practice of the daily Rosary in our home at Les Buissonets. But any external manifestation of Thérèse's love for the Mother of God could be only a very pale reflection of her close union and deep intimacy with the one whom she lovingly called " Maman."

It was to Mary that our Thérèse used to recommend all her personal needs and petitions. She confidently believed that any conversions which she might be praying for could be obtained by persevering recourse to Our Lady. At three o'clock, one afternoon, when I found her in prayer, she explained that she had formed the habit of reciting a *Hail Mary* whenever she took up her handiwork anew. In this way, she would be certain, she added, that all her labours would be consecrated to Our Blessed Lady.

I should like to add that our Mistress urged the novices to wear their rosaries around the neck during the night.

* * *

Towards the end of her life, Thérèse said to me one day, " Before I die, I want to write a poem which will transcribe my whole thought on the life and virtues of the Blessed Virgin."

Why I love Thee, Mary, a long epic based on the Gospel-text, was the crowning of this desire. The Saint completed it in May, 1897, four months before she died. Not only her whole thought, but also her whole heart and soul went into that Marian poem, the last poem Thérèse was to write on earth.

CHAPTER V

FRATERNAL CHARITY

FRATERNAL charity, with its wide range of possibilities in the Christian economy, was one of Thérèse's favourite themes. She left no stone unturned, therefore, to impress on her novices the supreme importance of this virtue in community life.

On this subject of love of one's neighbour, she shared with me a salutary lesson which she had drawn from the fifty-eighth chapter of the prophet Isaias:

> " Is this such a fast as I have chosen: for a man to afflict his soul for a day? . . . that he put on sackcloth and ashes? Wilt thou call this a fast and a day acceptable to the Lord? Is not this rather the fast that I have chosen? Loose the bands of wickedness, undo the bundles that oppress, let them that are broken go free, and break asunder every burden. Deal thy bread to the hungry, and bring the needy and the harbourless into thy house; when thou shalt see one naked, clothe him, and despise not thine own flesh." [1]

Saint Thérèse believed that this admonition should be interpreted in terms of man's moral

---

[1] Cf. Isaias LVIII, 5, 6, 7.

life, also. She perceived clearly that it is part of human nature in its over solicitude for the bodily necessities of the neighbour, to overlook his moral needs at times.

"We are surrounded continually by multitudes of souls in need," she told me, "by weak souls and souls that are sick and oppressed . . . Oh! to relieve them of their burdens and send them away free!" There are many ways in daily life of following this counsel, Thérèse pointed out, and an excellent opportunity is offered whenever the defects of others are spoken of in our presence. "On such occasions," she said, "be careful not to add a word as a sign of approval, but endeavour tactfully to point out some particular virtue of the sister in question; not, however, in an attitude of contradiction for this would be equally offensive to charity."

"*Free those* that are oppressed," she went on, "and break asunder the burdens of others. Deal thy bread—that is share your substance with the poor, with those who know not where to go; be prodigal to them, open up your house and part with your possessions. In other words, make a complete sacrifice of your rest and tranquillity."

After quoting the remaining verses of this passage from Holy Writ [2] the Saint continued:

---

[2] "Then shall thy light break forth as the morning, and thy health shall speedily arise, and thy justice shall go before thy face, and the glory of the Lord shall gather thee up. Then shalt thou call and the Lord shall hear: thou shalt cry, and He shall say, ' Here

" Oh ! when we consider the reward of all this effort ! The prophet promises that *you will recover your health* of mind; your soul shall no longer languish, and your justice will go before you." Thérèse then explained that by charity in word and by a sweet and affable manner we may even *break the chains of souls in captivity*: and by giving assistance to the poor and forlorn, by unselfishly making their sufferings our own, we merit the glorious reward promised by the prophet. These works of mercy, however, must remain hidden if they are to be meritorious, " like the humble violet," she said, " completely concealing the source of the marvellous fragrance it is shedding abroad. It is then that *the glory of God will envelop you*, not your own glory, you see, but the glory of God."

" *And the Lord shall hear you, and He will give you rest; a light shall rise up for you in the darkness*

I am.' If thou wilt take away the chain out of the midst of thee, and cease to stretch out the finger, and to speak that which profiteth not, when thou shalt pour out thy soul to the hungry, and shall satisfy the afflicted soul, then shall thy light rise up in the darkness, and thy darkness shall be as the noon-day. AND THE LORD WILL GIVE THEE REST CONTINUALLY, AND WILL FILL THY SOUL WITH BRIGHTNESS: AND DELIVER THY BONES, AND THOU SHALT BE LIKE A WATERED GARDEN, AND LIKE A FOUNTAIN OF WATER WHOSE WATERS SHALL NOT FAIL." (This last passage—in capital letters—was subsequently chosen as the *Benedictus Antiphon* for Saint Thérèse's liturgical feast).

" And the places that have been desolate for ages shall be built in thee; thou shalt raise up the foundations of generation and generation: and thou shalt be called the repairer of the fences, turning the paths into rest." (Isaias LVIII, 10-12).

and your darkness shall be as noon-day." This further promise delighted the Saint. She explained that although the darkness will not be entirely dissipated (for the soul is never completely freed from trial in this life) the *night shall be illuminated* . . . a light shall always shine in the midst of the interior gloom, and we shall have peace and joy. The soul shall then be *like a watered garden and like a fountain of waters whose waters shall not fail*; others will be free to come and drink at this fountain without harming it in any way.

The final recompense spoken of by the prophet? "The places that have been desolate for ages shall be built up in thee: thou shalt raise up the foundations of generation and generation." "How," Thérèse asked, "in this practice of charity and love of our neighbour can places be built up in us? What is the application here? Well, I like to think," she went on, "that by our hidden acts of virtue, by this practice of fraternal charity, we are known in heaven (according to the closing words of our text) as the *repairer of the fences* and that we are *turning the paths into rest* . . ."

The Saint watched me expectantly and intently during this meeting. "How mysterious it all is," she remarked, "that *from afar* we might, in this way, be converting souls and be bringing assistance to missionaries. It is more consoling than anything else, however, to think that on the Day of Judgment we shall hear it said of us that we have raised up material *dwellings* for Jesus and have prepared His Ways."

* * *

It would be impossible to enumerate the countless acts of charity which I saw Thérèse practise at Carmel. I honestly believe that she did not allow even one opportunity to slip by. For example, she thought nothing of giving up her free time on Sundays and other holydays in order to make others happy.

The Sisters often requested her to write some verses for special occasions, and the Saint did her best to comply, even to the point of following at times the rather prosaic outlines of her innocent petitioners. The result was that, seldom having a moment that she could call her own, she was obliged to sacrifice many personal desires, such as not being able to copy those poems or hymns which had appealed to her, and having to pass over some helpful passages in her spiritual reading. One of the novices, however, who knew the Saint's preferences in this matter, ordinarily jotted down such excerpts for her without telling Thérèse beforehand that she intended to do so.

"On my way to Compline after evening recreation," Thérèse told me one day, "I used to leave our sewing-basket on a bench near the Preparatory. This kept it out of the way of any possible spiders in the passage-way. However, when I noticed later that some other sister frequently dropped her basket there before me, I thought to myself, 'Evidently, this *is* a convenient spot, and in the future, I shall leave the bench free to make it easier for Sister in every way.'"

We cannot too often repeat that our Saint was ever on the alert for such acts of virtue, trifling in themselves it is true, but great because of the love which always prompted them.

*   *   *

In order to encourage me in the practice of virtue, Thérèse confided to me one of the sacrifices she was called upon to make during her first years at Carmel. As one of the former prioresses could not endure any fragrant odour, the Saint, in deference to her, had always been very careful not to have any sweet-smelling flowers, even so much as a tiny violet, at her cloister-shrine of the Child Jesus.

It happened that, one day, just as she was about to place a lovely rose before the statue of the Holy Child, she heard this Mother calling

her, and Thérèse knew why. " At that moment,"
my humble little sister confessed when relating
the incident to me, " I had a strong desire to let
this good nun go ahead and actually complain
before I should tell her that it was only an
artificial flower. But at the same moment, Jesus
was tugging at my heart for a sacrifice of this
little selfish satisfaction, and He won out.
Holding up the flower, I exclaimed gaily: ' See,
Mother, how well they imitate nature nowadays !
Wouldn't you think that this rose had just been
freshly gathered from the garden ? ' . . . Oh !
if you only knew how happy I was after that act
of charity, and how marvellously it strengthened
my character."

* * *

One day in the Infirmary during her last illness,
my sister called my attention to the soft, downy
linens which the infirmarian, Sister Stanislaus [3]
always had at hand for the benefit of her patients.
" Souls should be treated with the same tender
care," the Saint said, " but why is it that we forget
this so frequently, and allow those about us to
go on unnoticed in the endurance of sharp,
interior pain ? Shouldn't the spiritual needs of
the soul be attended to with the same charity,

---

[3] Sister Saint Stanislaus who died in her ninetieth year in May
1914.

with the same delicate care which we devote to
our neighbour's bodily necessities? For some
souls are really sick; there are many weak souls
on earth, and *all* souls without exception suffer
at one time or other during life. How tenderly
we should not only love them but also *show* our
love for them."

*   *   *

Whenever she happened to find any sister in a
disagreeable mood or at fault in any other way,
Soeur Thérèse would extend herself to be only
the more amiable, obliging and affectionate; in
this way she endeavoured to restore peace to an
agitated heart which, she knew, must be suffering. Her own goodness of heart, moreover, was
translated into a great visible tenderness to those
who, having pained her, had come to ask
forgiveness. One day in a conversation with me
on this subject she exclaimed:

"Oh! the unfathomable tenderness of God's
exquisite mercy towards the weak and imperfect.
I marvel when I see how He always seems to
surround them with His protecting love. We
should react in the same way to the peculiar
needs of our neighbour. Even in nature we have
a faint image of this provident concern of the
Creator when we compare the coarse bean with
the little green pea. Although both must endure

alike the heat of the day and the chill of night, yet the attractive little pea, you will notice, has not received the extra protection of the tough outer covering of the unattractive bean. Therefore in imitation of Our Heavenly Father let us also bestow a more indulgent love and protective care on those who have the greater need."

* * *

Believing that I was too self-centred at times, our dear Saint said to me one day: " This tendency to fall back on self makes the soul barren and incapable of the practice of virtue and whenever we find ourselves a prey to such self-introspection, we should have immediate recourse to external works of charity. At such times God does not require us to remain in our own company," she continued, " and for this reason, He often permits us to become obnoxious to ourselves precisely that we might get away from self. Our only escape, then, is to go on a visit to Jesus and Mary by the performance of charitable works."

* * *

I had confided one of my difficulties to her, and to prove that self-mastery had not always been an easy thing for her, she related the following incident to me:

It happened one night during the Great Silence that she was called on, as Second Portress, to prepare a night lamp for some visitors who were lodging in the out-quarters of Carmel. " What a bitter inward struggle I was enduring," she confessed, " nothing was at hand, the nuns had already gone to their cells, all office doors were locked. I was grumbling interiorly about circumstances and creatures, and was particularly annoyed with the Extern Sisters who had thrust this duty on me during our rest hour when they could have so easily taken care of the lamp themselves. Suddenly, however, divine light invaded my soul, and I was inspired to place myself at the service of the Holy Family at Nazareth. Then when it was question of preparing this night lamp for the Infant Jesus, I went about the duty with *so much love*, such great love, that it was with light step and a heart overflowing with fervour and consolation that I went ahead and completed my task.

" Ever since that memorable night," Thérèse added, " whenever I find myself in a tight spot I have recourse to this practice and it never fails to restore my peace."

* * *

Our Mistress said to me one day: " Your programme of life seems to be this: I will be kind to those who are kind, and amiable with the amiable. Then, naturally you become agitated as soon as someone disagrees with you. In this you are like the pagans spoken of in the Gospel. And Our Lord Himself tells us not to imitate them but rather ' do good to them that hate you and pray for them that persecute you.' To do good to those only who are good to us springs from a wisdom that is merely human: in other words, all for self and nothing for God."

*   *   *

It was a natural penchant of mine to want perfect order in all things, but more especially in the over-all routine of my daily life at Carmel. I cherished the ideal, at least theoretically, of bringing all my actions and the events of my life together as a unit, to fit in place like the pieces of a child's jig-saw puzzle. It is hardly necessary to add that such an outlook, besides being a source of conflict with others, was to provide me with many jolts on the way.

To give but one example. On a certain afternoon, during my sister's last illness, when I had been counting on finishing some particular work, I was unexpectedly called to the parlour. Later I told Thérèse with a sigh, " That unfortunate interruption prevented the completion of my task ! " She looked up at me and replied: " At the moment of death, such an interruption will

be seen in a very different light. You will thank
God for it."

* * *

My day of recollection each month meant
much to me, and I felt that I was entitled to a
fair amount of tranquillity and order at least
during that brief period of solitude. Hence, it
became for me something of a problem to
decide which Sunday would be best for this day
of retreat; an emergency in the Infirmary could
arise at any moment, and then there was always
the possibility of my being pressed into service
for some duty elsewhere in the monastery. As
this desire for a calm recollection was fast
becoming a besetting anxiety with me, Thérèse
spoke to me about it one day. She said:

> " It looks as though you go into solitude for
> your own gratification, and to give an extra
> little present to *self*. It should be the other way
> around. I take my day of retreat each month
> in a spirit of fidelity to grace and in order to
> give more to God. If, for example, I have a
> fair amount of writing planned for that day, I am
> careful to keep my heart detached, and I reason
> along these lines: ' I am putting such an hour
> aside for this task, but in anticipation, I offer
> up that hour to you, my God. It will probably
> be punctured by the many unforeseen inter-
> ruptions and disturbances which usually come

my way, so even now, I enter heart and soul into Your plan for me. In fact, I am really counting on being upset and inconvenienced, and if it should turn out that I am left at peace, I shall thank you, my God, for such an unexpected favour.' 'In this way', the Saint added, 'I am always happy and remain in great peace.'"

This advice was typical of Thérèse, and it was a grace for us to see how she used to put this very counsel to work in the discharge of her duties as Assistant Sacristan. On feast days, when she might have counted on catching up with some special work of her own, she was in the habit of passing the Sacristy from time to time (after she had finished her appointed tasks there) in order to give the first Sacristan an opportunity of pressing her into service again. Needless to say, this silent offer was often accepted.

Knowing that such extra duties must have been fatiguing, I devised a means of making it easy for her to slip away but my efforts were in vain. She was determined, it was evident, to refuse nothing to the good God.

* * *

One day in some matters of trifling importance I had given in to self on several scores. This was Thérèse's reaction:

"True, no serious harm has been done," she said, "nor has the peace of the community been disturbed, but there are some little ripples on the surface of your soul. We might compare it to the bruising of the downy texture of a little peach. To stand up for your own rights or to insist on justice being done is not necessarily a serious offence against your neighbour, it is true, but your own soul is the loser."

"What can I do, then, to make up?" I asked. "Just turn your eyes lovingly to Jesus," Thérèse answered, "and recognize your own misery and weakness. That is full reparation. You see, whenever we try to sustain our rights, it is only to our own spiritual detriment. You have no responsibility in the guidance of souls, so, to set about instructing others, even when truth is on your side, is exposing yourself to danger unnecessarily. You are not called upon to be a Justice of the Peace. This right belongs to God alone. But your vocation is to be an Angel of Peace."

* * *

Thérèse frequently urged us to practise great charity in judging others, for, as she used to point out to us, that which *seems* to be a fault in another is often an act of heroism in the sight of God. The unfinished task of a nun who may be over-tired or suffering interiorly, she told us, often brings more glory to God than a duty meticulously completed by another nun robust of soul and body. In other words, it is effort and not success that counts most with God. We should judge our neighbour favourably in every circumstance, therefore, and make it become a habit of our lives to overlook his faults. Just as we—almost spontaneously—give ourselves the benefit of the doubt, let us also make this an integral factor of our relations with those about us. And if, in a given case, we cannot ascribe a charitable motive, we can always have recourse, the Saint concluded, to an interpretation like this: Although Sister X is obviously at fault, evidently she is not conscious of it. If I, on the other hand, have clearer light in the present case, all the more reason why I should use much care in judging her mercifully and myself more severely for my inclination to blame her.

Thérèse believed that God frequently allows us to experience in ourselves the same weaknesses which we deplore in others, such as absent-mindedness, involuntary negligences, an attitude of boredom or weariness. When we see ourselves fallen into those faults we are then more prompt to excuse them in others.

With such an excellent guide, I learned how to see beneath the surface of circumstances and events, and a little experience soon taught me that often what I was prone to call an imperfection in others was merely an error in judgment on my part. I found that sometimes when I witnessed what appeared to be a failure in duty on the part of my neighbour, it was due rather to the fact that obedience, in the meantime, had imposed a more important or a more urgent task on the Sister. Moreover, she had only added to her merit by accepting in silence the humiliation of having, apparently, failed.

* * *

As we were walking in the garden one day, Thérèse said to me as she pointed to one of the fruit trees:

" Those pears aren't a bit attractive at present, are they? In the fall, however, when they are stewed and served to us in the refectory, we shall find them to our taste, and it will be hard to connect them with the fruit which we are looking at now. That is a good reminder of the truth that on the Last Day, when we shall all be delivered from our faults and imperfections, those Sisters, whose natural qualities may now be displeasing to us, might appear to us as great saints. And we shall perhaps gaze on them open-mouthed in wonder."

CARE OF THE SICK

When I entered Carmel, I was placed on duty in the infirmary. None of the religious was seriously ill at the time, although several were in a state of languishing weakness. One Sister in particular, afflicted with chronic brain anaemia and with the mental vagaries which mark this disease, provided her infirmarians with endless opportunities for the exercise of perpetual patience. This religious had adopted the principle that " at all costs the novices' spirit should be tried and tested." Her attitude was, alas, often translated into action, and the unfortunate situations arising from this extravagant behaviour can be better imagined than described.

It sometimes happened, for instance, that in answer to my bell, I would hasten to the Infirmary from the other end of the monastery only to have this Mother tell me: " My dear little Sister, I could hear you coming; why must your step be different from that of your companions ? "

One day, when I could stand it no longer, I fled in tears to Thérèse who did her best to console and encourage me. I can still see her at my side (we were sitting on a trunk together) and I remember how lovingly she held me in her arms.

For me, however, there was no hope of a definite change, for it was my appointed duty to spend a good part of the time with the sick. But my heart was very heavy at times. I often found myself going out of my way so as not to pass the Infirmary, and I even went so far as to bend over while stealthily hastening by the windows of that wing of the monastery; I was convinced that the mere sight of me made this Mother believe that it was her mission to keep me in perpetual motion.

Although Thérèse had a comprehensive view of the situation and, at heart, was in complete sympathy with me, she said to me on one occasion:

> "You should purposely pass by the Infirmary to give the sick sisters an opportunity to ask services which might inconvenience you. And if at times you simply cannot stop to carry out their commissions, tell them so in an amiable way, and promise to return. You should show a cheerful attitude about all this in order to make your patients believe that they are doing you a *favour* in accepting your services."

The bell calling us to the Infirmary should be like a heavenly melody, Saint Thérèse said. "Whenever it summons you to duty," she told me, "be convinced that it is the very best thing that could happen to you at the moment: consequently, you should force yourself to desire it." One such act of love for God—especially when performed cheerfully or at an inconvenient time,—is of much greater merit, Thérèse taught, than all our most sublime thoughts; even writing the lives of saints or composing other spiritual works are of small value when compared with these little feats of self-conquest.

"Whenever your bell is rung, or when you are called to perform some disagreeable task for the sick," said Thérèse, "you should consider yourself as a *little slave* whom everybody has the right to order about. A little slave, you see, because one who is a slave never thinks she has any right to complain."

"That's all very well," I countered, "but you must admit that some of the sisters in the Infirmary call me for no reason at all. Is it any wonder that I flare up?"

"I realize just how much all this costs you," Thérèse replied, "but if you could only see the angels who, from heaven's height, are looking on as you struggle in the arena of duty. They only await the end of the combat in order to deck you out as people crowned the knights of old with garlands and trophies. Besides, since we long to become little martyrs, it is up to us to *earn* the palm. Remember too that these small contests, minor though they be, are not without merit. The *Book of Proverbs* tells us that ' the patient man is better than the valiant, and he that ruleth his spirit than he that taketh cities.' " [4]

Thérèse said that if she were to live longer, she thought she would be happiest in the office

---

[4] *Proverbs*, XVI, 32.

of Infirmarian. She would not ask for this duty, however, for fear of being too presumptuous. "If it were to be assigned to me," she said, "I should consider myself highly privileged. Yes, I should be exceedingly happy to be called on to help in the sick-room during my religious life. Without a doubt, this office calls for much abnegation, but I believe I could put all my love into the work simply by recalling Our Lord's words, 'I was sick and you ministered to Me.'"

Our Saint repeatedly urged me to cultivate an attitude of *love*, of great love, while taking care of the sick. She insistently begged me to try to foresee all the needs of the sick and to lavish all my tenderness on the infirm sisters as though it were Almighty God Himself whom I was serving. She was convinced that this office, more than any other post in the monastery, called for assiduous application and maternal kindness.

In spite of such enlightened guidance, I still found it hard at times to make my rounds of the infirmary during the evening hour of rest and later, after Matins. On one occasion, when I spoke of my fatigue to her, she smiled sweetly and said, "Now it is you who are carrying little cups from this place to that, but some day in heaven Jesus 'will rise up and come Himself to minister to you.'"

Our little invalid's last months on earth were nothing but a series of unmitigated sufferings, for serious complications had set in. In order to give her some extra care, therefore, I was often obliged to put off going to the community recreation at the usual time. Moreover, I was, naturally, more solicitous for Thérèse's needs than for those of the other sick Sisters, none of whom was as seriously ill at the time. The Saint was quick to notice this. One day she gently admonished me, " If I were in your place," she said, " I would do my best to go promptly to recreation, even though not strictly obliged to do so. And I would force myself to be more alert to the needs of the other patients here. To win additional grace for you, I would extend myself to make a thousand little sacrifices, and to practise self-denial at every turn. We should guard against selfishness even in the most trivial matters for, as the *Imitation* tells us: ' Where a man seeketh himself, there he falleth away from love.' "

" Now, I am facing death. But my life has been a happy one because I have tried to put self-seeking away from me. The only way to attain happiness is to know perfect love. And the only way to attain perfect love is to forget self entirely and never to seek gratification in anything."

ZEAL FOR SOULS

Thérèse entered Carmel to immolate herself for the salvation of souls, for all the needs of

Holy Mother Church, and in particular to pray for the sanctification of priests. She was on fire with desire to sacrifice herself for these ministers of the Lord, for these " other Christs." She liked to repeat that when we pray for priests we " do business on a large scale," for it is through the head, that we reach the members. This desire to help priests by prayer and through them to save souls was in truth the object and aim of her life. Her letters to me while I was still at home are telling proofs of this burning ideal which she ever cherished and which, happily, we shared in common.

In the novitiate, she taught us a long prayer for priests which we often recited. She did not know who had written it, but later I learned that it is to be found in a publication entitled *Une Ame Sainte: Thérèse Durnerin.* [5]

---

[5] Although this subject (the sanctification of priests) played an important part in Saint Thérèse's entire life, Soeur Geneviève does not enlarge on it here inasmuch as most of Thérèse's observations and comments bearing on this theme have already been published in *The Collected Letters of St. Thérèse of the Child Jesus.* Sheed and Ward, New York, 1948.

The following are some excerpts of the prayer of Thérèse Durnerin: " . . . O Eternal Father, may our earth be impregnated by that ocean of love gushing forth from the opened side of Your Jesus that it may bring forth holy priests, priests who like John, the Beloved Disciple, will gather up the Precious Blood in their chalices on the altars. Send us priests who will give You to souls with that plenitude of love which the Apostle John received as a pledge of tenderness at the foot of the Cross . . .

" May your priests protect with jealous love Your Bride, the Church, just as St. John protected Mary, Your Mother, and took her unto his own. Instructed by this tender Mother of Sorrows

In order to give a feast-day gift to our Prioress, Mère de Gonzague, I took a special photograph of the Saint one day in June 1897. It was Thérèse who chose the setting for this picture; she wore her white mantle and veil and held in her hand a parchment on which were printed the words of Saint Teresa of Avila: " I would give a thousand lives to save even one soul." [6]

* * *

During our pilgrimage to Rome when Thérèse was only fourteen years old, I saw her put aside a missionary almanac after she had read only a few pages. " I had better not go on with this,"

---

on Calvary, may these priests watch over Your children with the exquisite tenderness and care of a Mother. May they lead souls on to intimate union with You through Mary who, as the Gate of Heaven, is the sole dispenser of the treasures hidden in your Adorable Heart.

" O Mary ! transfixed beneath the Cross by the sword which pierced the Heart of Your Divine Son . . . teach us how to please Jesus; let us run with you to His assistance when we hear His cry: ' I thirst ' . . . that cry which you heard at the foot of the Cross as He was expiring . . . Oh ! give us priests, on fire with zeal, true children of Mary, who will give Jesus to souls with the same tender care with which you carried the Infant Jesus of Bethlehem.

" . . . Mother of Sorrows ! . . . give us a generation of priests formed at your school and imbued with the tenderness of your virginal heart."

[6] This picture which was taken in the monastery garden did not turn out well, and the negative was destroyed. Nevertheless, copies of this photograph are in circulation in various parts of the world. In the picture, Saint Thérèse is standing next to a little table in the garden. (Translator's note.)

she told me, "for it might only intensify my yearning for the life of the missions. I have deliberately sacrificed it for the hiddenness of Carmel, where I can suffer more through the monotony of an austere life and thereby win more souls for God."

* * *

In her autobiography the Saint gives a graphic picture of her *Pranzini* experience, her persevering prayer for the conversion of this hardened assassin and the joy of learning that the criminal showed definite signs of repentance as he climbed the scaffold.[7] She had wanted to have a Mass offered for this "conversion" but as she was too embarrassed herself to give her confessor the Mass-stipend, I carried out this commission for her. She had not told me whose "conversion" she had in mind, but was relieved on learning

---

[7] Saint Thérèse had asked God for a *sign* of Pranzini's conversion and she tells in her *Life* how her petition was granted. An excerpt of an account of Pranzini's execution published in the French paper *La Croix* on September 1, 1887 gives the details:

"The Chaplain walked in front in order to hide from the criminal the sight of the fatal guillotine; the assistants help Pranzini along, but he repels both priest and executioners. He now stands before the machine. He is pushed forward and thrown on to it, and the assistant on the other side draws his head under the knife . . . But before the death stroke—it may be that a lightening flash of repentance penetrated his conscience—he asked for the chaplain's crucifix and kissed it three times. The knife fell, and when the separated head was held up to view, we thought: 'If human justice is satisfied, perhaps this last kiss will have satisfied Divine Justice also, which demands only sincere repentance?'"

that I had guessed that it was Pranzini. There-after, I became the confidant of her joys and hopes as the last weeks of the prisoner's life dragged on.

This zeal for souls began that memorable Sunday in July 1887, when at the sight of a picture of the bleeding Hand of Jesus Crucified, she felt the call to share in the Redeeming suffer-ings of the Saviour on Calvary.

At Carmel, where this desire for the salvation of souls could become only more intense and all-embracing, she was on the alert to make use of every opportunity, however trifling, to win souls to God. I recall one particular instance when Thérèse, in spite of her usual timidity, stealthily hid a medal of St. Benedict in the lining of a coat belonging to a fallen-away Catholic who was doing some work in our enclosure. He usually left his work-clothes in the monastery over night, and the Saint made use of his absence to perform her little act of zeal.

* * *

When the tuberculosis had spread to all parts of her body causing indescribable suffering, we were imploring heaven one day in tears to give our dear little sister some relief when she said to us: " I am asking God that all the prayers being offered for me may serve rather for *the salvation of souls* and not for the alleviation of my sufferings."

And I can still hear her declare:

> "No, I never would have thought it possible to suffer so much . . . never, never! I can only explain it by my intense desire *to save souls*."

This was one of her last confidences.

On many occasions and in different ways, Saint Thérèse promised that after her death she would "let fall a shower of roses." She was certain, it seemed, that she would be empowered *to do good* on earth even after she had entered eternity, that her prayers would assist Holy Mother Church, and that she would continue to work in her chosen apostolate, namely, that of winning many graces for priests.

Frequently, she returned to this subject and described in detail the nature of this "good," and the means she would use to bring souls to God, which was none other than teaching them her *way of confidence and complete self-surrender.*

Taking her up on one of these remarks, I asked her one day: "Then, Thérèse, you believe that in heaven you will be able to save a greater number of souls than if you had remained on earth?" She replied:

> "Yes, I do believe it. Why else is God allowing me to die when He knows so well how ardently I have desired to save souls for Him *in this life* . . . "

CHAPTER VI

FIDELITY TO THE RULE

SAINT Thérèse's esteem for our Rule and Constitutions was clearly demonstrated by her fidelity to the smallest point of our Carmelite *Way of Life*.

" How fortunate we are," she used to tell us, " that we have only to put into practice the code of laws which our holy Founders drew up for us at the cost of so much labour and toil ! "

She was visibly pained whenever she heard us objecting to anything that was laid down in our holy Observance.

* * *

Thérèse taught that in a community each Sister should try to take care of her own needs and not seek assistance except in urgent necessity. In order to preserve the golden mean, when there was question of asking a dispensation from a point of Rule or some extra work in common, she advised us always to ask ourselves, " What if all the nuns were to do the same? Your answer will show you at once," she said, " what great disorder would result, for we can always find enough specious reasons—in our appointed duties as well as in our self-chosen tasks—to be excused from work in common."

Our Rule and Constitutions specify the number of hours to be given to the Divine Office, to mental prayer, and to the community recreation, and these duties were particularly sacred to the Saint. She held that to infringe on even a small part of this time, in the interests of manual labour, was actually " stealing something from God."

Here Thérèse was our model in a special way. The first sound of the bell was the signal for her to cease all activity; the pen or the needle was put aside instantly.

She showed the same fidelity in her duty as bell ringer, when she would be seen at recreation folding up her sewing a few minutes before the end in order to go—even in the midst of an absorbing conversation—to ring the bell at the appointed moment. Practised over a long period of time, such constant self-denial is very mortifying to human nature.

In order to be present at Matins and other Community activities, Thérèse had to practice very meritorious acts of virtue.

During her postulancy and novitiate, unless she had received an express order to the contrary, she made it a point to conceal her ailments and indispositions, and at such times she showed greater vigour than usual. She never sought medications or other comforts and used them only when they were offered to her by those in charge.

Thérèse often suffered nausea while reciting the Divine Office in choir and her efforts to control it caused her to feel faint. This was the signal for her not to give in but to exert herself more. On these occasions she found strength in repeating one of her favourite sayings: " If I fall to the ground, I will surely be found." [1] She told me that this simple thought, which she often recalled, had really helped her in her religious life, especially in her earlier struggles.

* * *

One day when I was making a leisurely attempt to answer the signal which marked the end of an exercise, Thérèse said to me, " Hasten to your little duty and not to *your little act of self-love* . . . "

OBEDIENCE

Saint Thérèse's spirit of obedience was all embracing and it extended to every detail of her Carmelite life. She used to tell me, " We must never do anything to make the yoke of

[1] " Si je tombe, on va bien le voir ! " Words of a soldier when endangering his life to regain the flag. From a story Thérèse had read in childhood.

obedience easier for ourselves. We say we want to be martyrs, so let us use the means at hand and make our religious life a true martyrdom."

She followed this counsel in an heroic degree, and to the letter, in her own personal life. Superiors had to be cautious about recommendations made in her presence; for her, a simple suggestion from those in authority became an order. She remained faithful to such orders not only for a day or a week but over a period of a lifetime.

* * *

How I used to admire her as I watched her carrying out small recommendations, as for instance: to see that a certain door was always closed; to refrain from passing by a particular part of the Monastery; not to walk *through* the choir; and a thousand other little orders of our Prioress, Mère de Gonzague, who, incidentally, usually forgot, after a few days, that she had made these regulations. Reverend Mother did not realize at the time that this saintly soul considered her Superior's words as coming from the lips of Our Divine Lord Himself.

* * *

As a postulant Thérèse had been ordered by her Novice Mistress, Mère Marie des Agnes, to make known whenever she was suffering from a sick stomach. This condition occurred daily and the Saint believed herself obliged to make a regular report. Soon the Mistress, no longer remembering the order she had given, concluded, " This child does nothing but complain! " Thérèse submitted to the humiliation without any attempt at self-justification.

* * *

My sister made a complete sacrifice of her will, not only in the case of Superiors but of all the Nuns without exception—and for all time. One day, during her illness, the community had assembled in a hermitage to sing some hymns, and our Saint, wasted with disease, was obliged to sit down. But when one of the nuns made her a sign to stand, Thérèse, with an amiable smile, rose immediately and remained standing.

Later I questioned her about this as I could not believe that God had willed such an unreasonable act. " In matters of small importance," she answered quite simply, " I have made it a point to obey everybody, in a spirit of faith as though God Himself were manifesting His Will to me."

* * *

I had spoken rather sharply to a sister who had given me an unmerited rebuke. " She had no right to reproach me," I told Thérèse, " and, besides, it was not her affair ! " " That may be true," was the Saint's answer, " but Jesus has not said, ' *Obey your superiors only*,' has He? No, for He tells us: ' Give to everyone who asks of thee.' [2] and ' Whoever forces thee to go one mile, go with him two.' " [3]

A short time before her death, St. Thérèse said to Mère Agnes in my presence, " I have a little piece of advice for you: the Prioress should see to it that the infirmarians *oblige* their patients to make known their needs. This is very important, Mother."

She spoke about this to me also as it related to my duties in the infirmary. From this we suspected that Thérèse had been speaking from her own experience. Alas ! In her case it was then too late for us to do anything about it. Had we left her in want very often, we asked ourselves? Her sufferings in this matter are known to God alone, for frequently when we believed that we were giving her some relief, we were in reality only adding to her discomfort. [4]

The first Infirmarian, an aged nun who was hard of hearing, believing, on one occasion, that Thérèse was cold, whereas she was burning with

---

[2] Luke VI, 30.　　　[3] Matt. V, 41.

[4] The advice given by Saint Thérèse here pertains only to those who are *seriously* ill, for she more than anyone else in the Monastery had made her own our holy Mother Saint Teresa's recommendation (in our Constitutions); " Except when the malady is serious, let the sick cause as little trouble as possible to the Infirmarian."

fever, pulled up the covers over her patient's head. When Thérèse did not demur, the Sister then brought in more covers, and still the Saint submitted without a word. When I returned, I found my patient little sister drenched with perspiration.[5]

With a twinkle in her eye, she told me what had happened, and there was not a trace of annoyance in her voice. She assured me that she was happy " to accept this little hardship in *a spirit of obedience* to the first Infirmarian."

* * *

Saint Thérèse used to urge us often to be most faithful to the practice of asking the necessary permissions in our daily life. As a professed nun who had completed her probation she was, in reality, dispensed from the novitiate regulation of a weekly [6] renewal of all ordinary permissions. Nevertheless, she observed the custom until the end of her life.

" Rather than act without the blessing of obedience," she said to me one day, " at times I have done without something (even when I considered it indispensable), if I had forgotten

_____

[5] " Drenched with perspiration." Evidently the extra covers helped, at least, to break the fever. Did the first Infirmarian actually have such an end in view when she covered Soeur Thérèse in this way? (Note of Translator).

[6] Professed nuns at Carmel renew these permissions once a month.

to renew my weekly permissions. I was really scrupulous about this," she confessed, " and I was always interiorly disturbed whenever in an emergency I was obliged to proceed without the sanction of our Mother."

* * *

During the day, as she went about her duties, Saint Thérèse used to compose her poems but she did not put them on paper until evening. She might have obtained permission to jot down her verses as they came to her, but she felt that this would be failing in poverty as she did not consider her time her own.

" I had to wait, therefore," she said, " until our free hour between Compline and Matins, and sometimes it was extremely difficult to recall at eight in the evening the lines which had come to me that morning.

" These trifles are a species of martyrdom which we should welcome," Thérèse added. " It would be easy to avoid that pain if we permitted ourselves, or sought permission for, things that would make the religious life easier and more comfortable. Here we must give ourselves no latitude whatsoever." [7]

---

[7] Here Saint Thérèse has in mind that loving fidelity with which the Carmelite nun should observe the smallest rule of her Institute. It would be to misinterpret the Saint's thought to apply the counsel —" we must give ourselves no latitude "—indiscriminately, or in the unforeseen circumstances of daily life.

When she came to Carmel at the age of fifteen, Thérèse's childish penmanship bothered Mère Agnès. It would have been relatively easy for her to adopt a straight handwriting but she could not obtain permission to do so until the year 1894. Meanwhile the obedient child struggled on, trying in vain to improve her writing.

* * *

The ideal which our Mistress ever held up to us in the performance of our domestic duties was conformity to our holy customs. The natural urge to do better than others, an urge which is common to us all, often leads us into error, she told us repeatedly.

For example, in our private annual retreat when we are dispensed from all manual work done in common, we might feel inspired at times to assist the sisters who are folding the wet linen in the garret. It would be better, Thérèse held, to mortify this desire and follow our established custom—for two reasons. In the first place, other nuns during their retreat, while not having the same incentive, might feel obliged to follow your example, if they are to please God. Secondly, the extra obligation you have assumed might prove a burden when the fervour of inspiration begins to wane. In both cases, the result would be weariness and unnecessary fatigue.

We have all had the experience, Thérèse said, that the constant performance of the same action takes its toll on poor human nature. In the matter of voluntary practices, therefore, it is wise to take on only those duties which we can carry on perseveringly.

Another one of her counsels concerning monastic duties was this: whenever we are called on to give temporary assistance in another's office, even if we think we have a better method, we should willingly conform to the direction of the sister in charge. She has learned by experience the best way to do the work, and for us to impose our own views would be to hinder rather than to help.

* * *

POVERTY

I had copied some poems on loose sheets of paper and when one of the nuns asked to see them, I was not particularly pleased. "I should have a little more hope for their safety," I thought, "if I had only written them, like the other sisters, in a copy-book."

"You should be happy to be deprived of them," Thérèse told me. "Not only should you part with them joyfully, but you should even make it easy for the Nuns to ask for them again. If your aim in composing them was to do good to souls, you must go the whole way in the matter."

She added that in the interests of my little apostolate, I should be willing to be deprived of my poems entirely. Saint Aloysius Gonzaga, she said, in a spirit of poverty, made it a practice never to ask back any object he had merely lent.

* * *

" At one time," the Saint said to me, " you are complaining that somebody has upset your basket; at another, that you are in want of this or that. You should, rather, rejoice over these privations and remind yourself that since you are poor, it is only to be expected that you should be in want. You should tell yourself: ' These things are not mine anyhow and it is a blessing that they have been taken away from me.' "

* * *

I had been asked to give up a certain pin, and as it had been most useful, I missed it. " How very rich you are," Thérèse commented dryly, " You will never be happy ! "

* * *

" Have you ever noticed," the Saint asked me one day, " that normally most of us are quite willing to *give* with a generous hand? But to allow others *to take away* what belongs to us ! Ah ! therein lies the difficulty. Yet we have Our Lord's word in the Gospel: ' Of him that taketh away thy goods, ask them not again.' " (Luke VI, 30).

* * *

One day during her illness, I asked her to leave me a certain picture as a remembrance of her after death. " You are still harassed by desires, aren't you? " she said. " When I am in heaven with the good God, do not ask for anything that belonged to me, but accept with simplicity whatever our Mother might be inspired to give you. To act otherwise will prove that you are not stripped of everything. Then, instead of bringing consolation, the miserable keepsake will make you unhappy. Only in heaven shall we have a right to possessions."

* * *

A short time after Thérèse's death, one of the nuns offered to try to procure for me something which my sister had had for her use while still alive. Interiorly I asked the Saint to pass sentence on the proposal, and opening the Gospels to find her answer, my eyes fell on these words: " Like a man going abroad who called his servants and *handed over his goods* to them." (Matt. XXV, 14).

* * *

Because of her ardent love of God, Thérèse chose only the ugliest and most worn out articles for her personal use. I repeat that this stemmed from her love of God because by nature she was artistic and preferred objects that were attractive and in good taste.

One day when I unwittingly made an indelible mark on her sablier,[8] I saw the effort she made to accept this in silence and to try to conceal from me how much she felt the mortification I had provided for her.

* * *

She was ever aiming at a closer experience of true poverty; consequently, any privation that helped her along this road became a joy for her. Without giving in to a careless indifference, she never showed any concern about her appearance or whether she was wearing a habit that fitted her or not. Her clothes and even her hempen sandals were mended or patched until they were threadbare.

---

[8] A " sand-glass," used, at times, in Carmel in place of a clock or watch.

It was in this same spirit of poverty that she used carefully to scrape the gilt edges from the books and pictures which she had for her use.

When Thérèse's work basket had begun to fall apart, a sister drew it together with a band of old velvet which could no longer be used for any other purpose. Although extremely busy at the time, Thérèse removed the band and then replaced it wrong side out so that the basket might have a poorer and uglier appearance.

* * *

A novice had rubbed linseed oil over the cheap finish of her cell *ecritoire*, but immediately Saint Thérèse had her scrub it with a brush until every trace of the oil had disappeared. The furniture of the cell assigned to Thérèse had already been polished in this way by a former occupant; had it been up to her she would have restored the original finish without more ado.

* * *

On my entrance to Carmel, she passed on to me her own serviceable inkstand and holy water font and replaced them by others no longer fit for use which she had found in the garret.

I could not over-emphasize the point: the Saint kept nothing which she did not absolutely need and she always cast far from her anything that merely catered to convenience.

* * *

At Carmel she used a child's scissors which she had brought with her from home. This was often a source of inconvenience for her because of the various types of work to which she devoted herself in the community.

For several years of her religious life, whenever she wanted to use her cell-lamp, she had to take a pin to raise the wick and to push it down. But she always carried out this little rubric with such good humour that we came to consider the lamp as belonging to her; it looked as though she really preferred it to any other.

* * *

Whenever she could not take a borrowed pen-knife back to the art-room before retiring, she used to place it outside her cell-door. This was a silent indication that it was not among those objects which she was permitted to keep in her cell.

* * *

During her illness, when she was obliged to use a vaporizer for her feverish throat, the bottle which Thérèse chose for this purpose was fit for the junk-pile. Having accidentally broken it one day, in spite of my remonstrances, she resolved to acknowledge her fault in Chapter.

* * *

For the writing of her autobiography the Saint used two very cheap child's copy books which our sister Léonie, according to Thérèse's direction, had procured for her. At first she thought she would need only one, and she was very much surprised when she had to order a second.

For the pages addressed to Mère de Gonzague, Thérèse, then very ill, had to use lined paper. She was ordered, in view of her increasing weakness, to be less constrained and to leave larger spaces between the words and lines.

Her poems were scribbled on old envelopes or other waste paper—of all colours and sizes— which had been discarded. As a result some of her compositions were almost unreadable.

Saint Thérèse continued to use her pens after they had become unfit for service. Towards the end of her life when she was on a milk régime, she used to dip these pens into a few drops of milk " to sweeten their message," [9] as she used to say.

---

[9] " Pour les donner de la douceur."

Fearing that Thérèse's large crucifix would prove too heavy for the young child to wear constantly on her breast after Profession, Mère Agnès obtained permission to give the Saint her own smaller crucifix. My dear little sister who had always experienced a naïve delight in wearing *son grand crucifix* (even at home) told me, later on, how much this sacrifice had cost her. At the time, however, she had made no objection, and went on wearing the small one all through her religious life. It was this crucifix which she held in her hands when dying, and which may now be seen, with the Saint's relics, in *La Chasse* at her shrine in the Carmelite Chapel at Lisieux.

* * *

MORTIFICATION

Thérèse was always on the watch for those little acts of mortification which do not injure the health; these she practised consistently and at all times. True, such practices of self-denial are small in themselves, but does not the omnipotence of God shine forth in *all* the works of His Hand, the infinitely small things as well as those that are great? I have always maintained that Thérèse's greatness stems from the multiplicity of her microscopic acts of virtue, if I might express it in this way.

She told me one day that from her earliest childhood she had always felt an instinctive repugnance for the idea of taking her meals. She could never understand, she said, why the word "invited" should be used in connection with such a lowly task, why a banquet should be the chief drawing card to a social gathering.

"How strange," she used to say, "that when we want to spend time in another's company we usually invite them to dinner. We should, rather, be embarrassed when taking our meals and desire to be alone. Ah! if Our Lord and Our Lady had not taken these daily repasts while on earth I tell you that I could never have become reconciled to doing so myself."

However, during her last illness when she began to have some slight preferences for certain foods, she said to me rather sadly one day, "How much all this humiliates me! Nevertheless, I accept it in penance because I realize that God wills me to have some experience of this weakness of human nature."

* * *

Questioned as to her manner of sanctifying her meals, she answered, "In the performance of this lowly action especially, we should unite ourselves wholly to Our Blessed Lord. Very often it is in the refectory," she went on, "that the sweetest aspirations of love come to me. Sometimes I am brought to a standstill by the thought that were Our Lord in my place, He would have partaken of these same dishes which are being served to me. He would have taken whatever was offered to Him . . ." She loved to think that during His lifetime, His food was like ours. " Surely the Blessed Mother must have made soup for Him at times," she told me, " and I'm sure that, like us, He lived on bread, fruits, vegetables, fish, and all the rest."

It was with such thoughts as these that she occupied herself when in the refectory, and it was evident that during her meals, she gave herself over entirely to aspirations of love.

* * *

With regard to her food, she was not allowed to practise any self-denial but she made up for this by little acts of mortification in other ways while taking her meals. For example: if the handle of her knife or spoon had not been sufficiently dried, she allowed them to remain sticky and went through the meal using them freely without moving a finger to dry them. This mortification, she said, *lui coutait beaucoup*.[10]

One year, during the last weeks of Lent, Thérèse told me that it went so against her to

---

[10] " Was very difficult for her."

go on eating while a book on Christ's Passion was being read in the refectory that she took her food as though by stealth. As for water and other beverages which she might find at her place she would lift the cup furtively to her lips when there was a pause or when the subject matter of the reading was less moving.[11]

She related this to me not as an act of mortification to be copied, but in proof of her compassion for Our Lord's sufferings and death.

* * *

There were some special little rubrics which, in her childlike way, she used to carry out during meals, and quite simply she gave us this account:

> "I imagine myself at Nazareth in the home of the Holy Family," she said, "and if, for instance, I am served salad, cold fish, wine, or anything else pungent in taste, I offer it to the good Saint Joseph. Hot portions, ripe fruits, and the like are for the Blessed Virgin. To the Infant Jesus goes our feast-day fare, in particular, puddings, rice, and preserves. Whenever there is a wretched dinner, however, I think to myself cheerfully: 'Today, my little one, it is all for you!'"

---

[11] The text adds that Saint Thérèse said she did not have the same obligation to drink her beverage (un soulagement) as to take her food.

Thus in many gracious ways did she hide her mortifications. However, one day when our Mother had ordered a special dish for Thérèse, a novice found her seasoning it with wormwood because it was too much to her taste. Another time I saw her drinking horrible medicine very slowly. "Hurry," I urged her, "drink it off at once." "Oh no!" she answered, "greater penances are forbidden me, so won't you let me profit by these small opportunities?"

* * *

Our dear Mistress used to say that during recreation more than at any other time we should find opportunities for the practice of virtue. "If you desire to draw great profit from this exercise," she told us, "go with the idea of entertaining others and not of enjoying yourself. Know beforehand, that you must practise complete self-denial and detachment."

For example: I might be relating to a sister a story which I believe is interesting. If she interrupts me to relate something else which bores me, I should try to be interested, Thérèse counselled me. "Be careful then, not to try to resume what you were saying," she added, "and in this way, you will leave recreation filled with great interior peace. Because there was no self-seeking on your part, you will find yourself endowed with fresh strength for the practice of virtue."

" If only," Thérèse sighed, " we could realize how much we gain by self-denial in all things! "

" You realize it, certainly, for haven't you always sacrificed your own self-interest? "

" Yes," she replied, " I have forgotten self, and I have tried not to rediscover myself in anything."

In that one sentence, we have a picture of the true Thérèse. She practised self-abnegation with so much ease that no one would have suspected it was not one of her natural virtues, but rather the effect of her heroic correspondence to the grace of God.

This is just one example among many. When I was speaking to her one day about the impatient longing which some of us experience at recreation to give out a bright saying or to impart some unusual spiritual light, she told me that she, too, also suffered this temptation. I was not surprised to hear her say this, for I knew that with her keen mind, the quick, pointed repartée must have often died on her lips.

* * *

In our visits to the parlour, Thérèse would speak only when directly addressed. She practised this reserve to such a degree that even some of our close relatives imagined her to be rather unintelligent. Having entered religion too young, it was said, Thérèse's education had been *tronquée* [12] and she would suffer the effects of this all her life.

* * *

When the four of us were together one day during her last illness, Thérèse said: " When I am gone, take care that you do not lead a family life here. Without permission, do not tell one another what takes place in your visits to the parlour; in fact, do not even ask such permission except when there is question of something useful and not merely amusing."

* * *

In the matter of visits to the parlour, whenever she foresaw any gratification for self, she always tried to steal away quietly. She did not have to be urged to stay, on the other hand, whenever there was question of spending herself for others.

* * *

Whenever Saint Thérèse was ill she used to say so very simply—in obedience to Reverend Mother's order. As far as she was concerned, however, the matter ended there. Then it made

[12] Checked.

but little difference to her whether she was cared for or not. If it happened that she was not given the proper remedies, she took this as a sign that God was sure of her. Therefore, she received this divine compliment with holy pride and childlike joy.

* * *

She used to tell me: " Keep yourself interiorly detached and free from any piece of work you might be doing. Always let the nuns give you advice and suggestions about it and do not object if they touch it up, even in your absence. Naturally, because of differences of taste, they might, in this way, spoil it and you will begin to count as wasted the hours you have devoted to it."

Even if the work in question became worthless because of this interference, she said, the fact that I had been able to remain detached should make me very happy. " The goal of all our undertakings should be not so much a task perfectly completed but the accomplishment of the will of God." [13]

---

[13] To another novice who showed but little concern about her exterior duties, the Saint recommended assiduous application of mind and heart. This is only another proof that all souls cannot practise these counsels indiscriminately. At the time, moreover, Soeur Geneviève's chief duty, as a novice, was concentration on her interior life.

In order to afford her some relief one day during her illness, I thought out a plan which I brought to completion so speedily and (in her estimation) so ingeniously as to give Thérèse cause for no little astonishment. After she had complimented me for my cleverness and charitable promptness, she said, " I wonder if there would have been such alacrity on your part had somebody else—say, for instance, the first infirmarian—ordered you to do this."

The Saint went on to develop her thought in this way. Whenever there is question of relief or alleviation for those in need of it, we usually look favourably on such exceptions if it is we who have been instrumental in procuring them for others. But let somebody else take the initiative, then we are tempted on all sides, finding countless " ifs and buts " as to the lawfulness of these dispensations.

" We find it so easy," Thérèse concluded, " to find fault with anything exceptional when it has not come within the sphere of our own influence."

* * *

Saint Thérèse's spirit of detachment was always in evidence whenever the community gathered together to be photographed. As it was my part to prepare the camera and place the nuns in proper position, I usually found it impossible,

at the last moment,[14] to join the novitiate group
gathered around our Mistress.   Naturally,
Thérèse and I desired to be together—in some
of these pictures at least. She told me, before
she died, how much it had pained her at times
that the novices had not been on the alert to make
this possible. On only one occasion, however,
did the Saint decide to do anything about it.
One day when we were being snapped while
at the wash in the laundry, she asked Soeur
Marthe de Jésus to let me have her place—which
was next to our Mistress.

She had an extremely affectionate heart.
Ordinarily, however, it was only when her
sisters were alone with her that she gave proof
of her great love for us.

Having read that in their desire for greater
perfection, some of the saints had thought it
necessary to cut off as much as possible all
contacts with their relatives, Thérèse often told
us that she found great comfort in the thought
that there are many mansions in our Father's
home in heaven. " Mine," she added, " will be
not with the great saints but with those little
saints who always retained a great love for their
family."

When we were conversing together about her
possible departure for the foreign missions,

---

[14] When an elderly nun, who did not wish to be photographed,
would usually take over.

however, and I asked what could be her motive in wanting to go, she replied, " It is not because I expect to be of any service to the Carmel of Hanoi but simply that I might *suffer exile of heart*."

* * *

During the years when my duty to our sick father kept me in the world, Thérèse often became uneasy about me and feared that I could not escape being influenced by the social environment in which circumstances had placed me.[15] On one particular occasion, when I had to go to a ball, my little sister became unusually perturbed and summoned me beforehand to the Carmelite parlour. She told me that she had been weeping as she had never wept before— and then proceeded to lecture me. Nevertheless, believing that her precautions were a little exaggerated and that, in this instance, she was too severe, I asked her whether she wanted me to make myself ridiculous?

Thérèse answered rather indignantly: " O Céline, remember the three young Hebrews who preferred to be thrown into the fiery furnace rather than bend the knee before a golden statue. By your vow of chastity,[16] would you imitate

---

[15] Céline and her invalid father spent a good part of their time at the Guérin's hospitable and beautiful " Chateau de La Musse."
[16] Céline had made this private vow while still in the world.

the folly of the times and adore the world's golden statue by giving yourself over to dangerous pleasures? Take heed of the warning I am giving you on the part of God." She begged me to consider the reward He bestowed on those young men, and to strive to follow their example. However, as I was obliged to go to the ball, I had to pray for much light and grace. I had resolved not to dance, and wondered how I was going to manage . . . Carrying a large crucifix, I set out finally for the " soiree," keenly aware that my relatives were going to take offence at my unusual behaviour. During the evening, after I had already refused several pressing invitations, I was suddenly swept on to the dance floor by a *gallant Monsieur*. Strange to tell, it became impossible for either one of us to begin the first step of the waltz. There was a minor mystery about it all: at each new musical measure, my embarrassed partner made another attempt, and although I did my best to co-operate, it was all in vain. At last, with solemn step, he led me back to my place, and then quietly slipped away. Personally, I was not at all abashed. In fact, I was experiencing an inward joy as I laughingly related my experience to the staid ladies who had been looking on, enviously. My little misadventure, I think, brought some balm to their hearts!

I had been finding the religious life rather hard on nature, and some months after my entrance, Soeur Thérèse tried to encourage me in this way:

> " You say that it is the sacrifice of your will that is costing you so much, but is it really true that you are not doing your own will at Carmel? In the details of daily living, yes, but was it not because of a deliberate choice on your part that, in the first place, you adopted this mode of life ? "

She then explained that I was actually doing my will by renouncing it, because I was well aware of the renunciation required of me when I sought admittance to the cloister.

" As for me," Thérèse added, " I tell you I could not remain one moment in the monastery through constraint. No one could ever force me into a life like this. In choosing it, therefore, with my eyes wide open, I have subscribed by anticipation to all contradictions which shall come my way in the religious life, to all that goes counter to my will."

The Saint then reminded me that this is the meaning of the public declaration which we make on our Profession Day, namely, that " it is of my own *free will* that I desire to be a Carmelite."

One Sunday in March 1895, while walking with the novices in the garden, I spied a little white snowdrop in one of the flower beds. As I leaned over to pluck it, Soeur Thérèse held me back with the words, " We're not allowed to do that! "

That I was no longer free to pick even a tiny flower was too much for me, and my eyes filled with tears. Later, in an effort to find some comfort, I went to our cell and tried to write a canticle which would remind Jesus of all I had given up only to find it again in Him. However, the words would not come, and the poem consisted of this line alone:

> " La fleur que je cueille, o mon Ro ,
> C'est Toi." [17]

Some days later, Thérèse who had shared this little experience with me brought me a poem which she had written for my consolation. It was entitled *La Cantique de Céline*, and was published later as *Ce que j'amais*.[18] In each verse, the remembrance of some particular sacrifice which I had offered to Christ was matched by the hope of a compensating joy in eternity. The entire poem is a telling reminder of Saint Thérèse's complete detachment from the things of this world.[19]

---

[17] " The flower I pluck, my King, is Thee."

[18] *What I Used to Love.*

[19] The following are selected from the fifty-three verses which she wrote on this occasion.

> Oh ! how I love your memory
> My childhood days ! so glad and free.
> To keep my innocence, dear Lord for Thee
> Thy Love pursued me night and day
> Alway.

Thérèse's spirit of renunciation was as constant and consistent as it was based on common sense. I shall give here some examples of her acts of self-denial; in a number of cases I was an eyewitness and at other times, the Saint related the incidents herself in order to urge me on.

During her absence from recreation one day, a letter was read in which there was mention of Thérèse. Later, she asked me to let her see it, and with permission, I passed it on to her. Some

> I loved the distant hills, the plain,
> The waving fields of wheat, the grain.
> My breathless joy when in my sisters' train
> I'd pluck through many hours
> My flowers.
>
> I loved the swallow's graceful flight,
> The little dove's low chant at night,
> The pleasant sound of insects—gay and bright
> The grassy vale, resounding long,
>   Their song.
>
> Lord ! now I am Thy prisoner here
> Gone are those joys once held so dear.
> I have found out—none last, all seek their bier
> I have seen all my joys pass by
>   And die !
>
> In Thee ! I have the springs, the rills
> The mignonettes, the daffodils,
> The eglantine, the harebells on the hills
> The trembling poplars, sighing low
>   And slow.
>
> My joy is Thee ! each hour increased
> My God ! and I though last and least
> Would leave this exile for Thy Heavenly Feast
> And sing my love, upon Thy Knee,
>   For Thee.

days later, I asked her if she had found it interesting, and she confessed that she had not read it. When I pressed her to do so, she would not so much as open it as she had resolved to punish herself for having asked for it in the first place. It was this type of mortification which appealed to her in a special way.

Unless charity required her to do so, Thérèse made it a point, when going about the monastery, to avoid joining any group of nuns to whom the Prioress might be communicating some current event. She always did her best to remain in complete ignorance of the news of the day.

* * *

Soeur Thérèse saw one of her most cherished dreams realized when I entered Carmel on September 14, 1894. The fact that she would be able to guide me along her Little Way made her supremely happy. Nevertheless, as I crossed the threshold of the cloister, her first act was one of renunciation. After the older religious, she embraced me in her turn and had already left the group when our Prioress, Mère Agnès, made her a sign to go to our cell and await me there. As Assistant Mistress and also as " angel "[20] she was entitled to this privilege, but would not avail herself of it on her own initiative.

---

[20] Angel—the Sister appointed to assist the postulant during her first bewildering days in the monastery.

Likewise, when our community welcomed our cousin, Marie, as a postulant (August 15, 1895), Soeur Thérèse with the other younger religious was standing at a little distance from the cloister door. One of the nuns called to her to come closer to catch a glimpse of the relatives who were at the enclosure entrance, but the Saint remained where she was.

A year had passed since we had seen the Guérins for their regular visit. Later, I reproached Thérèse for not having taken advantage, like her three sisters, of this opportunity, and she answered that she had acted in this way to mortify herself. She admitted, however, that she had felt the sacrifice keenly.[21]

* * *

During the hour of prayer and at other community exercises, Thérèse, like the rest of us, was tempted at times to glance at the clock. She used to check this inclination by reminding herself, " Although I am hard pressed for time, I will not be any better off by knowing how much longer I may have to wait." So she would kneel on in patience until the bell signalled the end of the choir duty.

---

[21] The glimpse, at best, could be had only through the black veils which covered the faces of the religious on this occasion. . . . During the preceding year, the parlours were under construction, which precluded the regular visits.

As Assistant Turn Sister, the Saint practised angelic patience with the good old sister in charge, who was slow in her ways and rather eccentric. In winter, when Thérèse's hands were always chapped and covered with chilblains, this aged sister reserved to herself the privilege of wrapping the inflamed fingers in multiple little bandages. One day, as I was noting compassionately that there was only one spot still visible—on the little finger—Sister X proceeded to bury that joint also. Seeing my bewildered expression, Thérèse laughed heartily.

* * *

One day during her illness, we received a small box of *dragees de baptisme*.[22] As, customarily, these were souvenirs everyone wanted to see we brought them to the Infirmary. In our excitement, however, we forgot to show them to Thérèse. She was careful not to remind us of the oversight although the box was resting on a table not far from her bed.

* * *

In order to give spiritual help to a companion in the novitiate, Thérèse adopted a programme

---

[22] Sugar-coated almonds or small candy pellets. These are packed in little white boxes and given as souvenirs of an infant's baptism.

which was in little accord with her personal
inclinations. In this daily round of practices, the
two novices used to offer the Infant Jesus at one
time a fragrant flower or delicious fruit, at
another, some attractive article of clothing or the
like. Frequently, they entertained Him with a
concert, choosing different instruments which
would suit a particular feast or mystery.

My sister entered into this contest with such
good grace that her companion became convinced that it was Thérèse, and not herself, who
needed these external helps on her road to God.
Needless to say, the novice was mistaken for such
a set of practices ran counter to the Saint's
definite attraction to a life of simplicity.

* * *

Walking with her in the garden one day early
in my religious life, I offered Thérèse some
petits frisants de la vigne.[23] To suck these little
vine leaves had been one of our childish delights
at Les Buissonets. She refused them, however,
saying that she had denied herself this small
satisfaction during her religious life. As it was
a feast day, I thought it made a difference and
tried to insist, but to no avail. " I have promised
Little Jesus," she said, " that henceforth I would
taste ' les frisants de la vigne ' only in the kingdom of His Father."

---

[23] Young vine shoots or tendrils.

In spite of this spirit of constant self-denial, there was nothing narrow or straitlaced in the Saint's understanding of the virtue of mortification. For example: from the window of the cell assigned to me on my entrance to Carmel, the railroad could be seen in the distance, and very simply Thérèse made the remark, " I'm sure you will like to see the trains speeding by."

She made no allusion to the opportunity I had of depriving myself of this innocent pleasure. But God took care; shortly after my entrance, a new building rose up which almost entirely blocked out my view of the railroad !

In the practice of mortification, Soeur Thérèse never went in search of the extra-ordinary, nor did she have any inflexible rules about the enjoyment of legitimate pleasures. In this as in everything else, she acted with great simplicity, and was eager to *bless God in all His works*. With this end in view, she liked to touch the velvety texture of various fruits, especially the peach, and she did not hesitate to breathe in the fragrance of the violet and the rose—all flowers, in fact, to such an extent that she was able to identify the particular perfume of each species.

Nevertheless, as soon as she became aware of any purely natural pleasure, she would desist at once. On her deathbed, she could remember only one infidelity in this matter: while in the world, she had taken a momentary pleasure in the scent of some *eau-de-Cologne.*

* * *

Before she became a religious, Thérèse deliberately turned away from the use of penitential instruments; as a Carmelite, however, she was most faithful to the bodily austerities prescribed by the Rule. As to the voluntary corporal penances which were practised in the monastery, she also embraced them generously until, as she relates in her autobiography, she fell ill from wearing for too long a time a little iron cross on her breast.[24]

For my part, I had found by experience that even in the matter of voluntary bodily austerities, human nature has subtle ways of diminishing the pain. When I spoke to Thérèse about this, she answered, " The way I look at it is this. My only reason for undergoing any corporal penance is to inflict extra pain on the body—as much as I can possibly bear. So why by some ruse of poor human nature should I allow myself to be led into ways of lessening the pain? "

---

[24] At the Canonical Process, Mère Agnès testified: " During this illness, Soeur Thérèse told me that God had enlightened her on this subject of corporal austerity. If she had become ill for so trifling a cause, she said, she took this as a sign that extraordinary penances were not meant for her or for those ' little souls ' following her on the path of spiritual childhood."

However, she had seen for herself that the most penitential religious are not necessarily the holiest, that self-love finds, at times, great satisfaction in these excessive mortifications. This more than anything else alerted her to their danger. And she often reminded us that all bodily penances are nothing when placed in the balance with charity.

* * *

Shortly before her death, I learned that when Thérèse was a novice, one of the sisters, while helping to fasten her scapular at the shoulder, accidentaly ran the large pin through the skin. For severall hours, the Saint joyfully endured the pain in silence.

CHAPTER VII

FORTITUDE IN SUFFERING

ALTHOUGH Saint Thérèse was harassed by temptations against faith during the last eighteen months of her life, in her conversations with the nuns she never made any reference to this interior suffering. Her perfect conformity to God's will in this trial was reflected in a serenity of countenance and cheerfulness of manner which led the community to believe that she was walking in the way of spiritual delights. Only those who knew her intimately understood her agony of soul.

At various times during the course of this long spiritual night, I feel certain that she longed to pour out her heart to me in the hope that this might bring her some interior relief. However, the fear of communicating to me the contagion of doubt in such grave matters held her back, and she carried her cross alone.

Occasionally, when I questioned her about the trial, she would gaze at me profoundly and answer, " Ah! if you only knew! . . . I would not want you to suffer these temptations for even five minutes."

Sometimes, in the midst of a casual conversation, she would make a slip, and ask in plaintive tones, " Tell me about heaven," or again, " Does heaven really exist? "

In glowing terms, I would then proceed to remind her of the joys of eternal life and the Beatific Vision. Usually, there was no response except at times a disconsolate " Ah! . . . " I was not slow in realizing that my words of comfort were only augmenting her sorrow and more often than not, we had to change the conversation.

Oh! how I suffered as I witnessed Thérèse struggling daily with this heavy cross. As she was only too well aware of the fact that I was powerless to help her, she frequently pleaded with me at least to pray for her.

At the beginning of this trial, when she spoke of her temptation to the community confessor, Reverend Père Godefrey Madelaine,[1] he counselled her to copy out the Creed and wear it over her heart. She wrote it in her blood. It will be remembered that it was during this period that she composed some of her most inspiring poems on eternal beatitude, in which she expressed, as she tells us, only what she believed in *naked faith*. On the surface, she was experiencing nothing but doubt, anguish and darkness.

---

[1] It was to this priest that Soeur Thérèse's *Histoire d'une Ame* was given for examination before it was published in 1898.

She met the assaults of the enemy by frequent recitation of the act of faith, and after a long siege, came through the trial victorious. Her sublime ecstasy at death bears eloquent testimony to this truth.

* * *

As the work of purgation went on in my soul, I began to understand that the death of the " ego " meant the sacrifice not only of natural delights but of spiritual joys as well. In my early religious life, this was a devastating experience. I had to face the truth that I could no longer expect to *feel* those ardent and zealous impulses of Divine Love which had urged me on in former days.

Thérèse, on the contrary, lived, like our holy Father, Saint John of the Cross, " appuyee sans aucun appui," [2] but at the time, I was not attracted by such austere maxims.

" In the world," I told her, " I was so inflamed with zeal that there was nothing I should not have attempted for the glory of God. For love of Him, I was willing to face wild beasts, and I yearned to travel to the ends of the earth to make Him known. Whereas now, all this enthusiasm of love seems to have died away; I have courage for nothing ! "

---

[2] " Securely stayed yet without stay."   First line of a poem entitled *Gloss on the Divine* by Saint John of the Cross.

" That's a sign of youth," answered the Saint.
"True courage does not consist in those momentary ardours which impel us to go out and win
the world to Christ—at the cost of every
imaginable danger, which only adds another
touch of romance to our beautiful dreams. No,
the courage that counts with God is that type
of courage which Our Lord showed in the Garden of Olives: on the one hand, a natural desire
to turn away from suffering; on the other, in
anguish of soul the willing acceptance of the
chalice which His Father had sent Him."

*   *   *

Thérèse said to me one day: " People in the
world think that we religious have very little to
suffer, that our sufferings are, at most, only petty
ones. '*A la bonne heure,*' they say. ' It is the trials
we laymen meet with in everyday life which
really deserve the name of crosses.' "

The Saint agreed that while the ordinary
Christian is beset with grave trials during life,
the cross of the religious usually consists of
countless daily pin pricks.

However, as she pointed out, even though the
layman's life may be one long series of crosses,
the religious, by his consecration to God, has
definitely entered on the *way* of the cross, without hope of truce or respite. All things being
equal, a spirit of greater endurance is required

of him. To carry his cross patiently is not enough; his goal embraces also the ultimate purpose of the cross, namely, the destruction of the " ego," the conquest of self.

Experience proves, she said, that the minor trials of religious life have often succeeded in vanquishing souls who were known in the world for their virile courage, who had borne the death of parents, children, and loved ones with remarkable fortitude of soul.

" I have seen for myself," Thérèse added, " that often it is the nuns who apparently have the strongest natures who are most easily overcome in little things—so true is it that the greatest of victories is the conquest of self."

" It is all too true," I exclaimed, " and this self-denial in little things is too difficult for me. I'll never make it! I see clearly what I ought to do, I promise to do it, and then at the first encounter, I am overcome." " The reason for that," she replied, " is that you have not softened your heart *beforehand*. Whenever you are annoyed with a nun, the best way to regain your peace is to pray for her and beg God to reward her for making you suffer.

" Sometimes it happens," she went on, " that despite their best efforts, some souls remain imperfect because it would be to their spiritual detriment to believe they are virtuous or to have others agree that they are."

The Saint was of the opinion that our type of cloistered life, cut off as it is in every way from the active apostolate, can be a kind of crucifixion to human nature. To go on working for God without encouragement or distraction of any kind, never to see the fruit of our labours, and to concentrate on the overcoming of self, was, she thought, the sacrifice of sacrifices.

* * *

During my postulancy, I was assigned to work in the habit room, and was also on call for some duties in the Infirmary. Over and above these tasks, I was often pressed into service in the art department; in fact, I had begun to do some painting as soon as I entered Carmel. First, it was a medallion for a chasuble, then I was asked to use my brush on countless little objects for the Prioress' feast of Saint Agnès.

As it was *ma premiere d'emploi* [3] who had arranged this extra work for me, I went ahead with a certain amount of docility, although my preference was for sewing. It was not long, however, before Sister X, perceiving that my work in the habit room was being neglected in favour of my artistic accomplishments, began to scold. This, I might remark, is one of the little " crosses " to be met with in religious life. I was crestfallen and poured out my heart to Thérèse.

[3] The sister in charge in the habit room.

To console and encourage me, in the name of the Blessed Virgin she wrote a poem which I found in my slipper after Christmas Midnight Mass. At the time, my name was *Marie de la Sainte Face*. The following verses tell the story.

> Do not become disturbed, Marie,
> About your daily duty's score.
> Your only task on earth shall be
> To love your Jesus more and more.
>
> When others, as they will, complain
> That you have nothing much to show
> For all your work. Take heart again!
> LOVE is your talent here below.

In her effort to comfort me, my Little Thérèse had admirably succeeded!

*   *   *

One day the Saint said to me, " I have always noticed that I have a great capacity for suffering and very little for rejoicing. Joy seems to take away my taste for food, whereas on the days when I have much to suffer, I have a ravenous appetite. It is a fact that my system cannot take too much joy."

Although ardently desiring martyrdom, she did not seek suffering for suffering's sake; it was for her the best means of proving her love for

Jesus. In this, she was like Our Lord Who, in order to show His love for us, longed for His baptism of blood while at the same time dreading it in His Human Nature.

Furthermore, while she often told Our Lord how much she desired to suffer martyrdom for Him, she always subordinated this prayer to the designs of Providence on her soul. To the very end of her life, this disposition of total abandonment to the divine good pleasure was the predominating force in her life. She gave expression to it in these words:

> " I desire neither suffering nor death although both are dear to me. Abandonment alone is my guide today. I can no longer ask for anything with great ardour except the perfect accomplishment of God's will in my soul."

* * *

Thérèse's interior mortification was so pronounced that she could never bring herself to ask God for the smallest consolation. A little story will illustrate how she tried to impress me with this idea of unselfish love for God.

During the first years of my religious life, although I was struggling continuously, there were innumerable defeats and but few victories to my credit. As a result, I was almost always discouraged. While I found it easy to grasp the wise counsels of my dear little sister, this made things only worse because I saw that I was not translating them into practice in my daily life. Often I said to myself, "I'll never have the courage to persevere to the end in this striving for perfection, and since I am not capable of greater effort, I'll make my act: less merit for all eternity!" [4]

In my dilemma, I went to the Blessed Virgin one day, asking her to give me some ray of hope; my prayer was followed up by a consoling dream.

I seemed to be out in our garden quadrangle, downcast and in tears. It was as though I were enveloped by the vast expanse of sky, and as I raised my eyes, I saw numberless little clouds on all sides. These were interwoven by crowns, thousands of them, resembling haloes surmounted by stars. As the clouds dispersed, the crowns multiplied.

I stood there spellbound and my tears vanished . . . I also noticed that the horizon was red, blood red, and that gradually the crimson glow was rising upwards.

Even in my dream, I was stirred by a realisation that I had been called to Carmel not for my own happiness or satisfaction but solely for the glory of God; I was to sacrifice my life for others, and win heaven for sinners. As a mother of souls, then, I would travail in sorrow.

---

[4] "And a little more peace of heart on earth." Though not included in the text, this sentence or its equivalent completes Soeur Geneviève's thought.

My heart was throbbing with joy at the thought
of such a sublime vocation, and I awoke in a
thrill of happiness. Hastening to my dear little
Mistress˙ to tell her about my dream, she said,
with some animation, " Oh ! that is something
I would never do . . . ask for spiritual consolation. You say you want to follow my way. Well,
you know how often I repeat:

Fear not, O Lord, I shall awake Thee . . .
I await in faith the happiness of heaven.

" It is so sweet to serve our Lord in the night
of trial; we have only this life to practise the
virtue of faith! . . . "

*　*　*

In her last illness, she was far from being led
by the way of spiritual consolations. She said to
us one morning after Communion, " It is as
though they had put two little ones side by side.
They are very quiet. Once in a while, I whisper
something to Jesus, but I get no answer. Doubt-
less, He is sleeping! "

*　*　*

I was complaining on a wash day of being more
tired than the other nuns. Besides the ordinary
work, I had several additional duties unknown to
the rest.

"You should act like a valiant soldier," Thérèse said, "never grumbling at hardships but looking on your wounds as mere scratches; the type of person who is always ready to bind up the minor cuts of others, considering them more serious than his own."

After she had worked on me for a few moments, I was ready to agree that I felt my fatigue so much only because others did not realize how tired I was . . . Our lack of courage, as she said, often springs from a disappointment that nobody is pitying us. She continued: "Sometimes at the mere words: 'Go and rest yourself, Sister, you are so worn out,' the nun in question will immediately feel somewhat refreshed . . . To desire that others should know about our aches and pains places us in a class with *le vulgaire*.

"Saint Margaret Mary Alacoque relates that once when she had two whitlows, it was the hidden one that gave her the greater pain; the whitlow which was visible to all was, in part, soothed by the pity and compassion of the other sisters."

Thérèse had much to say on this subject which might be summed up in this way: When you are pitied, be consoled; when you are neglected, rejoice . . . Reach out to the sufferings of others and convince yourself that they have greater need than you to be pitied and consoled.

When I told her one day that unforeseen duties had been preventing me from profiting by my free time on Sundays and other feast days, Thérèse answered, " My Sundays and feast days are the days when I have greater trials."

* * *

Soeur Thérèse always saw things in their true light. She never got excited. Whenever you went to her for direction, you were sure of receiving sound, solid advice. It was evident that she did not act on impulse, and she possessed remarkable self control.

She used to urge us to wait until we had regained our self possession before going to her to confide our temptations and grievances. If, however, she saw that we were too wrought up to wait, she would consent to hear us out.

" Never speak about any unpleasant situation, even to our Mother, for the sole purpose of having it remedied," she told us. " Open your heart, rather, through a spirit of duty and detachment of soul. Whenever you realize that you are not in this frame of mind, it would be better to wait until your soul is at peace. To speak out, even when it is only a tiny spark of resentment that you feel, will only serve to add fuel to the fire."

At all times, Thérèse's countenance reflected the peace and tranquillity of her soul, and she wanted to see this serenity in her novices. She did not like to see us knitting our brows; to her this was an indication of some small interior anxiety.

Nothing, I repeat, could make her agitated or excited; rumours of persecution or other threatened calamities inspired her only with a greater spirit of gratitude to God.

* * *

One day, we were having an entertainment for Mother Prioress' feast and the Saint was representing Jeanne d'Arc at the stake. Through an act of imprudence on the part of another, the thing caught fire, and our Mother, in order to protect her, ordered Thérèse not to budge. While the nuns were trying to smother the flames which were crackling at her feet, my dear little sister stood there perfectly calm while offering the sacrifice of her life to God, as she told us later.

* * *

In all the minor accidents of daily life, while trying to repair the damage done, Thérèse always remained perfectly calm. Shortly after my entrance to Carmel, however, I almost succeeded in upsetting her equilibrium when our inkwell overturned. When I saw blotches of ink on our whitewashed wall and all over the floor, I ran to her in distress, " Come *quickly*," I pleaded.

When she saw me, she could hardly keep from laughing. True, I was a sight to behold; at the time, I was wearing the large white crepe veil over our postulant's bonnet.

Smiling sweetly, she said, " Don't worry, everything will be all right. I must admit," she added with a twinkle, " that your veil looks like *cloth of ink* ! But we'll soon get it back to its original colour."

Then, without any undue haste, she had everything restored to its normal state in a short time. I was astounded as I saw how calm she could remain in the face of these unforeseen accidents in life.

* * *

She was deeply pained, however, whenever she had an accident which involved a fault against poverty.

On February 2, 1897, eight months before her death, as server in the refectory, with the edge of a tray she knocked the serving window glass and broke it. As she was already in a suffering state, she could not control her tears, and began to cry.

While helping her to pick up the pieces of glass, after the community had left the refectory, I tried to console her and she answered, " Today being the anniversary of my dear little brother, Theophane Venard, I had asked Our Lord to give me something big to offer in his honour. Well, of myself, I would not have chosen this sacrifice because of the fault against poverty. Nevertheless, as it was a pure accident, I am offering it up as an incense of sweet odour."

*   *   *

INSTRUMENTS OF GOD

Thérèse was my ideal and I often told her how I longed to imitate her. I was always bringing new problems to her and she was able to give the enlightenment I needed to set me on the path of truth.

" You know very well," I used to say to her " that God has a special love for you since He entrusts souls to your care. He also inspires others with a love and esteem for you; there is no denying that the Community as a whole has confidence in you and bears you great affection."

" That makes no difference," she replied, " for I am really only what *He* thinks I am. As for loving me more because He has given me charge of souls, to be His interpreter to a little group of novices, I do not share your opinion. I think He has made me rather your little servant. It is *for you* and not for myself that He has bestowed those virtues which make me pleasing in your eyes."

She said that she compared herself to a little bowl of milk. All the kittens come to drink from it, and sometimes they quarrel about which one is to have the largest share. The Holy Child Jesus, keeping a sharp watch, says to them, " You may drink from My little bowl but I don't want it overturned."

They heed His warning! In any case, it would be difficult to break the bowl because it is already on the ground, as Thérèse observed, but the same cannot be said of Prioresses, she added. Although they also are vehicles of grace for others, they run a greater risk, as they are set up on pedestals. Honours are always dangerous.

" According to *your* needs," she said, " God pours out the milk into His little bowl. Yet you insist that He is favouring *me* rather than *you* by doing so."

I replied, " Nevertheless, you must admit that He has confidence in you, that He is sure of you . . ."

" Ah! you don't understand the matter," she told me, " for, humanly speaking, the privileged ones are those whom God keeps for Himself. Take for example two small pots of incense.

One He reserves for Himself, the other He lets exhale its perfume to the world. Which pot has received the greater favour?

" Again, sometimes we see pretty little baskets, tied with red or blue ribbons, which have been placed in shop windows to call the attention of the passer by. Does the decoration add anything to their real worth? Indeed not, those in the shop's closets are often more valuable; sometimes they are even prettier, for it requires a minor miracle for anything on constant display to retain its freshness and beauty. . . . And," Thérèse sighed, " this is what you are *envying* ! "

" Oh no! " I replied, " I am envying it only because *you* are the possessor."

" Suppose," she said, " that I were favoured with extraordinary graces. It would be a *venial sin for you to desire them*—even for that reason." [5]

I told her that under those circumstances, it would be difficult for me to suppress that desire. I realized that it was all childishness but I felt that if *I* were receiving extraordinary graces, I would rather be deprived of them if she were going another way. This of course stemmed from my confidence that God Himself would always direct Thérèse's steps on her path to heaven.

A soul is not holy, the Saint explained, just

---

[5] Cf. Saint John of the Cross—*Maxims and Spiritual Sayings*— No. 34. " The soul that desires revelations sins, at least, venially."

because Our Lord uses it as an instrument. Often, an artist is obliged to use a small brush of little value rather than other more expensive brushes within reach. The fact that he has used the small brush does not, however, add anything to its worth.

" We should try to grasp this truth," she added, " and attribute nothing of good to ourselves. No one actually possesses the virtues he practises, so let everything redound to the glory of God."

Thérèse was utterly convinced of these truths, and she was very fond of making apt comparisons on the subject. At one time, she spoke of the little spark which often starts a conflagration; at another, about the reading of some ordinary book which began a chain of conversions. She never tired of repeating, " God has need of no one, so let us not take foolish pride in the thought that He decides to make use of us at times."

* * *

The Saint used to make some remarkably wise and shrewd observations on the theme of sanctity and glory. She reminded us that we know some of the saints better only because they are nearer to us. This does not mean, necessarily, that they are the greater saints. Just as some stars which seem to us very small—and even those which we cannot see at all—are incomparably more beautiful than those which, to the naked eye, are " stars of the first magnitude."

On earth, she said, it is difficult to make a proper judgment in these matters . . . It is a fact that often as souls are ascending to the summit of sanctity, they even begin to *lose* the esteem of men . . .

" 'The canonized saints," Thérèse continued, " are not always those who are highest in glory. God has brought them forward for *His* glory and for our edification rather than for any personal honour." She had read somewhere, she said, that the love of the saints for one another in heaven will be measured not by their greatness or glory but chiefly by their mutual sympathy. " This makes it possible," she concluded, " that we can love all *little souls* with an affection greater than the love which we owe to the greatest saints. This thought fills me with delight."

Even in the matter of love and devotion, is it true to say that the canonized saints receive the greatest share because of their numerous clients on earth? Thérèse did not think so.

" Where is the saint who is loved just for himself? " she asked. " In this life is there any such thing as disinterested love? A certain saint might be praised, they write his life, and there is no end to the feasts and solemnities they prepare in his honour. Celebration follows celebration, there are fireworks, the devotees are in a delirium of joy.

"After the excitement has died down, those in charge of the celebration believe that all turned out well . . . *if* they were allowed to follow their own plans through to the end. For some time after, it is the organ or the choir or the wonderful preacher who is praised . . . And what about the Saint? *Ah moi!*" cried Thérèse, "give me utter oblivion rather than this *demi-gloire*. It is from God alone therefore that I look for any praise or glory that I might deserve."

The saints are not saints, she said, because we recognize them as such, nor have they become greater after their *Life* has been written. Who knows? The spiritual good derived from the reading of a given biography might very well be traced to the inspiration of some unknown saint whose prayers made the soul ready to be benefitted by the book. "I often think," she told me, "that maybe I owe all the graces I have received to the supplications of some little soul whom I shall know only in eternity. What great revelations await us in the next life!"

There are many Carmelites who have died as saints, she pointed out, who will hardly be remembered on earth because their circular letter or obituary notice was badly written—or not written at all. Other nuns, on the contrary whose virtue was quite ordinary, have been placed on a pedestal simply because the Mother Prioress who wrote their lives had a facile pen !

" How can we desire a glory like this," she smiled, " a glory that is sustained by a gossamer thread. It is more like a lottery. At least, so it seems to me . . . Were some of the saints to return to earth, I wonder how many would recognize themselves when reading what has been written about them." [6]

She liked to think, she said, that she would be loved by everybody in heaven, even by those who were not too fond of her on earth . . . The love which the saints receive from their clients in this world, she believed, redounds more to our happiness than to theirs; it is *we* who are gathering in the fruits, it is *we* who are profiting by our prayers to them.

" It is interesting," Thérèse said, " to see how in one *Life* a man will be praised because he was free from temptation, and in another biography, sometimes by the same author, a saint will be eulogized because he was constantly *fighting* temptation . . . Wherein then does true glory consist . . . Thank God I have never sought my own glory," she concluded. " My attraction was,

[6] At another time, Thérèse said to Soeur Geneviève, " All the saints in heaven are my relatives. As soon as I enter eternity, I shall make a curtsy to each saint and ask him to tell me about his life—not a long drawn out account but one that I can absorb in the twinkling of an eye."

rather, for contempt—until I realized that even that was too glorious. It was then that I began to yearn to be *forgotten*."

She added, however, that like me, she also had reached out at one time of her life towards the beautiful, the sublime, and the perfect; that she had often experienced a certain feeling of exile when, in her presence, others were praised for their accomplishments and she was made to feel that she was lacking in talents.

When I asked how she was able to rise above this feeling of discouragement, she answered humbly, " For a while, I was able only to *put up* with it in peace; then I tried to make myself love it, and now it is really sweet for me to feel it."

* * *

All through life, Soeur Thérèse felt instinctively that she would die young, and this helped her to spurn all earthly delights. The *desire* for death never left her. In fact, she made it the barometer of her love of God. Did she love Him as much as she used to love Him? Yes, if death continued to have the same attraction for her.

When things were going prosperously, or whenever some unexpected joy came into her life, she was always on her guard lest the present happiness might diminish this desire for death.

" Why should I be afraid of death? " she said to me one day. " During life, I have always striven to please the good God alone." And when somebody said to her, " Maybe you will die on a feast day," she answered, " I don't have to die on a feast day. The day of my death will be for me the greatest feast of my life."

* * *

To assure me of the unchanging happiness of heaven, Thérèse often repeated to me that God has arranged all things so well in eternity that the elect will have no reason to envy one another. She was intent on bringing home this lesson to me as may be seen by the following examples.

One day I was arranging some artificial flowers in her presence. After watching me for a little while, she told me that just as I had placed the smallest blossoms where they would show to best advantage,—for the most part in between the large beautiful flowers—so will it be in heaven. The glory of the greater saints will be enhanced by the beauty of " les petits," and vice versa.

As I put the finishing touches to my little bouquets, having freshened up a leaf or petal here and there, the artificial flowers had taken on a new look. Thérèse then pointed out to me that this was a striking example of what God will do for us all, after we have been relieved of the miseries of this life.

The Gospel of the workmen of the eleventh hour—who had received the same pay as those who had borne the heat of the day—delighted her. " See," she said, " if we place all our confidence in the good God, and constantly put forth our best efforts, while hoping everything from His Mercy, we too shall receive the reward of the greatest saints."

* * *

A friend had given me a nice little doll, and I decided to place it on the table for the feast of our Mother Prioress. Although it was all but lost among the magnificent works of art and needlework of the other nuns, my gift took the prize.

Thérèse told me that the saints—our elder brothers and sisters—will treat us in the same way. They will give us presents, and it is we who will be enriched. She added; " On the feast day table, there were splendid works of art and other costly gifts—the fruit of long patient hours of labour and study on the part of the nuns. To me these sisters are like the great saints who have performed wonderful deeds and who have left us their admirable writings.

" Yet, your little doll attracted greater attention . . . and it was a mere plaything that had been *given* to you. *Rien de vous!* " [7]

---

[7] " You had no part in it."

CHAPTER VIII

DEATH OF THE SAINT

THE Saint's last years on earth were the echo of her holy life. She seemed to radiate a kind of luminous peace, the reward, no doubt, of her faithful practice of filial abandonment to God, her unflinching patience and unalterable humility. She had, it was clear, reached at last the goal towards which all the ardent desires of a lifetime had been converging. Like Our Lord just before His death on the cross, Thérèse said very solemnly to me the day before she died: "All is well, it is consummated: it is love alone that counts."

The sufferings of those last months defy description. Pulmonary tuberculosis, gangrene of the intestines, and large painful ulcers had reduced her emaciated body to a pitiable state, all the more appalling because of our utter powerlessness to help her.

It was at this period that, as second Infirmarian, I was given almost exclusive charge of our dear little invalid. I had a cell adjoining her room, and except to give assistance to some other nuns in the Infirmary, I never left her save for the various hours of the Divine Office.

During these brief intervals, Mère Agnès replaced me in the Infirmary and it was in this

way that she was able to record some of the
Saint's last confidences and conversations. After
the Canonization, the major part of this diary
was published under the title of *Novissima Verba*.

It was in the early hours of Good Friday in the
year 1896 that a haemorrhage of the lungs convinced Thérèse at last that she was gravely ill.
Nevertheless, in spite of her condition she asked
and obtained permission to continue the Car-
melite-lenten régime as she had begun it—in all
its rigour. Never dreaming that she had had such
a serious attack I watched her admiringly as she
carried out the whole observance on those last
two days of Holy Week. It was only later that I
learned that the black fast had been particularly
difficult for her that year but, as was her usual
custom when life was hard, she had not com-
plained.

In the following months, when assistance at
the Divine Office—at an hour when her fever
was at its worst—had proved extremely fatiguing, she asked neither relief nor dispensation.
She was most careful, moreover, to conceal from
us at the time that taking part in the laundry
work of the community—doing the wash and
folding the wet linen—after that first haemorrhage was taking more out of her even than
assistance at choir. And what shall I say of her
courage in undergoing the various treatments
ordered by the community physician?

It was heart rending to see him use the cauterizing needle so freely on the wasted body of our little patient—one day, I counted more than five hundred applications. As he worked on our heroic Thérèse who had to stand and lean against a table during the process, he conversed with our Mother about the most trivial things. The Saint told me later that she used to offer these ordeals for the salvation of souls, and that it was a help, during these sessions, to dwell on the sufferings of the martyrs.

Without waiting for any word of sympathy, she left the room as soon as the treatment was over. Going up to her cell, silent and trembling, she would then sit down on the edge of the wooden plank of her bed, there to endure the long after effects of this drastic treatment.

As yet, she was not considered to be seriously ill. When night came, therefore, she had to sleep on her paillasse.[1] Not having permission to give her a mattress, I could only fold a blanket in four and place it under her sheet.

My poor sister always accepted this little attention with touching gratitude and no words of criticism or complaint ever passed her lips about the primitive way our sick Sisters were treated at that period.

It is true that in the most acute attacks of pain she always retained a sweet serenity and a child-

---

[1] A canvas bag filled with straw. Carmelites use this in place of a mattress.

like gaiety. This often puzzled me and more than once I was tempted to think that perhaps we were wrong in believing that she was suffering so intensely; I could settle this doubt, I thought, if I came on her in a moment of crisis. I did not have long to wait. A little later, when I saw her smiling angelically, I asked the reason.

"It is," she answered, "because the pain in my side is very bad at present; I have made it a point always to welcome suffering eagerly."

HEROIC CHEERFULNESS

To the end of her life, Thérèse retained those childlike and charming mannerisms which made her company so agreeable and attractive. All the nuns were anxious to visit her in the infirmary and to enter into conversation with her. This amiable cheerfulness seemed to take on a new dimension as her suffering increased. While it was only another manifestation of her fortitude of soul, it was also the effect of her exquisite charity: she sought in this way to lighten our poignant sorrow as we thought of the impending separation.

During these months, she multiplied her little pleasantries and dialogues with me, often making use of nicknames which touchingly recalled the memories of our childhood. While all this was chiefly for my amusement, it also served on several occasions, to drive home some necessary lessons to me.

I have no hesitation, therefore, in yielding up to the public an account of these delightful little experiences with Saint Thérèse wherein her simplicity contrasted so poignantly with her virile courage during the last agonizing hours of her life. It is now impossible to give any definite dates so I shall group these reminiscences together just as I remember them.

Among the stories which had gladdened our childhood, there was one concerning a young girl Mlle. Lili and her little brother, Monsieur Toto. Being older than Thérèse, I was Lili and she inherited Toto's rôle.

In order to divert my thoughts, frequently in the intimacy of Carmel, she alluded to our respective titles. For instance, one evening when she was over-tired and feared that she would not hear the signal for rising on the following morning, she said to me:

> " Will you please take a look in tomorrow morning to see if Toto has heard the clapper?" [2]

And again:

> " Don't forget to awaken Monsieur Toto tomorrow morning, poor Demoiselle Lili, humiliated by everybody [3] but dearly loved by Jesus and Toto."

---

[2] A wooden rattle used at Carmel as a signal for rising.

[3] Allusion to the customary humiliations by which novices are usually tested.

On the doctor's order, I was obliged to apply the cauterizing needle to Thérèse's back. I knew that in doing so I was inflicting torture on her (later she confided to Mère Agnès that it had been like a martyrdom for her) but she actually urged me on in the performance of this unwelcome duty.

On one of the scheduled days when I wanted to skip the treatment, Thérèse gave me this reminder:

> " I am afraid that if you omit the treatment you will displease our Mother for she is a staunch believer in these cauterizations *especially on the back*. When the doctor comes on Sunday, he will probably ask why we have not followed his directions . . . Maybe you could wait until Monday? Well, *Pauvre, Pauvre* [4] do whatever you wish; I shall be ready tomorrow however. Above all please do not speak to this poor Monsieur Toto." [5]

*   *   *

A novice had shown Thérèse a picture in an almanac, which represented a shrewd merchant addressing his friend.

---

[4] A name taken from a story.

[5] So as not to break the " Great Silence," when the treatment, evidently, was to take place. This Silence at Carmel is observed daily from the end of evening Compline until after morning Prime —7.30 p.m. to 7.15 a.m.

" I am rich, very rich! Yes, indeed, and when I began business, I had *nothing*! "

" Ah, true! " answered the other, " but when you began, the one with whom you were going to do business had something! " [6]

Our little Saint added, " Like this man, I am rich, very rich. Yes indeed, and when I began business, I had nothing. Ah! but the One with Whom I did business had something ! . . . . [7]

* * *

The Saint was always on the alert to give me lessons of self-detachment.   To this end she compared our journey throught life to that of two children whose pictures she had seen on a holy card. With their Guardian Angel protecting them, the little ones were standing on the edge of a precipice. The boy wore only a light tunic and was free from all encumbrance, save the grasp of his little sister's hand. The latter, however, was carrying a large bouquet and was on the point of bending over to gather more flowers within her reach.

The Saint made this application.

" Once upon a time there was a certain *Demoiselle* who possessed great wealth which was not good for her. But she valued it above every-

---

[6] In the text, the business man speaks with the accent of a French Jew: " Che suis riche, dres riche . . . etc."

[7] Thérèse affected the same accent here.

thing else. Her little brother who owned nothing fell ill. It was then that he said to his sister: " *Demoiselle*, if you are wise, you will throw all your riches into the fire for they really are a great hindrance to you. Then you may become my *bo-bonne* [8] and give up your title of *demoiselle*. And when I reach the ' enchanted land ' whither I am going I will come to fetch you because you shall have lived poor like me, without any anxiety for the morrow.

" The *demoiselle* knew that the little brother was right. She became poor like him, *acted* as his *bo-bonne*, and was no longer tormented by a desire for those perishable riches which she had thrown into the fire.

" Her little brother kept his word. When he arrived at the enchanted land, whose King was God and whose Queen was the Blessed Virgin, he came to fetch his *bo-bonne*. The two of them lived happily for all eternity on the throne which they had chosen—the very lap of the good God."

* * *

Another time, pointing to the same picture, and to that of a mistress of a home who had everything she desired, Thérèse teased:

---

[8] *Little Servant*, Thérèse's name for Soeur Geneviève, the second infirmarian. In the Saint's weakened state, *bo-bonne* came easier to her than her sister's religious name. She had humbly asked permission to use this nickname rather than that of *Céline*, which name she cherished to such a degree as to discard all calendars without the feast of St. Céline on October 21st.

" Overly rich *Demoiselle* ! Rose buds for her
lips, the songs of birds for her ears ! [9] Clothes,
kitchenwares, many little trinkets ! . . . "

As I slept almost in the same room with her
—in a kind of alcove—Thérèse often saw me lay
aside the clothing I wore while nursing her.   On
one of these occasions, looking with pity at me,
she exclaimed:

" *Pauvre, pauvre!* How shabby you are, but
it will not always be so. You can take my word
for it. " [10]

* * *

Thérèse always welcomed the thought of
death.   From it she was always seeking new
lessons to point out to us. For example:

" When I am dead—*un cadavre*—I will finally
be silent and no longer your counsellor. When
they are trying to move me from left to right,
I will not be able to lend a helping hand. They
will probably be saying, ' She looks better this
way ' (or that way), and I still shall not speak,
even were they to place burning coals beside
me . . .   This thought should detach us from
the petty disturbances that arise in this life,
from all that does not concern us. "

---

[9] Allusion to something the Saint had read about Theophane
Venard: " Il avait un bouton de rose sur les levres et un oiseau
a chanter a son oreille. "

[10] " Pauvre, pauvre, comme vous etes toree. " In the text, a
footnote explains: (*Mal tournee*) Tore, en latin, torus: corde. "
Thérèse was here repeating an expression she had heard somewhere.

As I have said, she rejoiced at the thought of her own death, and was happy to see (accidentally) any of the remote preparations we might be making—should an emergency arise.

A box of artificial lilies was delivered for her bier, and she asked to see them at once. " At last! they are really for me! " she exclaimed. She could hardly believe that this joy was at last within reach.

When death seemed imminent, the nuns kept the blessed candle, the holy water and sprinkler at hand in the Infirmary. One evening, Thérèse sensed that they were near, and asked that they be brought within view. From time to time, looking at them complacently, she said to us playfully:

> " When the Divine Thief comes to fetch me, put the candle in my hand. But not the candlestick, please. It is too ugly."

In a light hearted manner, Thérèse described all that was to take place after her death—all the details of her burial etc. In this way, she forced us to smile when we preferred to weep. In truth, it was she and not her sisters who created the cheerful atmosphere which prevailed in the Infirmary.

She was utterly detached from all earthly concerns. Shortly before her death, one of the nuns spoke in her presence about the purchase of a new enclosure plot in the Lisieux cemetery for our deceased sisters. Quite amused, Thérèse said to me later:

> "What difference does it make the kind of grave we have? Some missionaries have been eaten by cannibals, and the martyrs have often been buried in the bodies of ferocious beasts."

LAST EXCHANGE OF CONFIDENCES BETWEEN SOEUR GENEVIÈVE AND SOEUR THÉRÈSE

During Thérèse's last months on earth, Mére Agnès and I kept a record of the interesting and —at times—amusing incidents which took place during our visits with the Saint. While some of my notes refer to the same conversations published in Pauline's *Novissima Verba*, there is, here and there, a slight divergence of detail. This is not to be wondered at; the Evangelists themselves, while recording identical events in the Gospel, did not, it is clear, always take the same approach.

MAY

One day when I was with Thérèse in the garden, while she was still able to say the Divine Office in private, she became visibly moved. Placing her finger on a page of the breviary, her eyes filled with tears as she said, " See what Saint

John the Evangelist tells us in this lesson at Matins: ' My little children, I tell you this that you may not sin. But if we sin, we have an advocate with the Father, Jesus Christ, His Son.' " (John II, i).

JULY 3rd.

Milk did not agree with our invalid, and as she could not retain anything else at the time, Doctor de Corniere ordered a kind of condensed milk— " lait maternisé." For certain reasons, this disturbed Thérèse, and when the bottles were brought to the Infirmary, she began to cry bitterly.

Later that afternoon, in an effort to rise above herself, she said plaintively, " Please read me something from the life of a saint. My soul is in need of some strong food."

I asked, " Would you like something from Saint Francis of Assissi? He'll entertain you with stories about his little birds." Very seriously, she answered, " No, not for entertainment but to give me *some lessons in humility*."

JULY 12th

Our Mother Prioress could not resign herself to the thought of Soeur Thérèse's approaching death; consequently, she would not grant the Saint's request for " permission " to die. Referring to this in the playful manner she assumed whenever she wanted to distract us from our sorrow, Thérèse said,

> " The good God has such an ardent desire for a certain little bunch of grapes which the owner will not give Him that He will be obliged to come and steal it."

* * *

One of the sisters had remarked that, before death, Thérèse might experience an hour of fear which would help to atone for her sins.

" The fear of death to wash away my sins! " the Saint exclaimed. " That would be just as good as a stagnant pool . . . Nevertheless, should I finally experience this fear, I will offer it up for others. Then as an act of charity, my suffering will help to wash away their sins.

" *As for me, however, only the fire of Divine Love will cleanse me from my sins.*"

* * *

Gazing on me with compassionate tenderness my little Thérèse interrupted a conversation and said,

> " Ah ! it is my little Soeur Geneviève who will miss me most. Indeed, I pity her more than anyone else. For, whenever she becomes disturbed, she always runs to me . . . and soon I shall not be here when she comes . . . Well,

the good God will give her courage, and *I shall return*." Then addressing me directly, she promised, "I will come back for you as soon as possible, and for this I shall enlist Papa's aid. Remember how he never put off till the morrow that which he could do today?" [11]

As I went about the Infirmary speaking to her about the approaching separation, I heard her humming. In my name, she was singing this little verse which she composed as she went along:

Thérèse is mine; she's mine forever
Naught shall ever come between!
Life nor death the bond could sever
That joins Thérèse to her Céline.

A little later, she looked up at me and said, " Mon petit Valerien! "

(She always liked to compare our union of heart with that which existed between Saint Cecelia and Saint Valerian).

* * *

When I said to her, " After your death, God will not be able to take me to Himself immediately, because I will need more time to become perfect," Thérèse answered,

---

[11] On April 28, 1958, Soeur Geneviève entered her ninetieth year, having completed sixty-three years of religious life. This promise of Saint Thérèse, made in 1897, evidently underwent " revision " after she entered eternity where " one day is as a thousand years and a thousand years as one day."

"That will not hold Him back. The story of Saint Joseph of Cupertino is a proof. He was of mediocre inteligence—in fact, really ignorant. He could preach on only one passage of the Gospel, namely: 'Beatus venter qui te portavit.' [12]

"Happily, it was just that text on which he was examined for admission to the priesthood, and he spoke so eloquently that the ecclesiastical judges were lost in admiration. With great honour, he was then raised to the sacerdotal state together with his three companions. The latter were questioned only in a general way, for it was assumed that having been in Joseph's company, they were as spiritually enlightened as he." [13]

"Therefore," Thérèse added, "I shall answer for you . . . and the good God will give you gratis all that He has given me."

JULY 18th

I was reading to her about eternal beatitude when she interrupted me and said, "It is not that which attracts me . . ."

"What is it then?" I asked. "Oh! it is Love!

---

[12] "Blessed is the womb that bore Thee." (Luke XI, 27).

[13] Here Saint Thérèse's memory was at fault. The life of Saint Joseph of Cupertino which she had only *heard* read does give this incident—but *with modifications*.

To love, to be loved, and *to return to earth* to make Love loved." [14]

JULY 21st

While I was trying to put things in order in her sick room, she was following me with her eyes. Then rather suddenly and without any provocation, she said,

> " In heaven you shall take your place at my side."

Later she quoted a stanza from a poem on Louis XVII by Victor Hugo [15] and added, " *I shall give you the sky-blue wings of a rosy cherub.* [16] I shall fasten them on you," she insisted, " for you would not be able to do so yourself; you would place them either too high or too low."

JULY 24th

I told her, " You are my ideal, but an ideal I shall never be able to attain. It is really pathetic," I added. " I am like a little one who has no sense

---

[14] In those last months of her life, Thérèse seemed to be haunted with the desire to come back to earth after death. It was constantly in her thoughts, and, at times, she would ask, anxiously, if such a hope was valid. When her sister, Soeur Marie, saw her one day in March 1897 praying in Saint Joseph's hermitage, and asked the object of her petition, Thérèse answered that she was asking Saint Joseph to beg God to grant this favour.

[15] Vous viendrez bientot avec moi
     —— bercer l'enfant qui pleure
   Et dans leur brilliant demeure
   D'un souffle lumineux rajeunir les soleils . . .

[16] This remark was prompted by something in Hugo's poem.

of distance; resting in the mother's arms, it puts out a little hand to catch something only to find it beyond its grasp."

" That may be true," Thérèse replied, " but on the last day, God will place within the reach of His dear Céline all that she could ever have wished for—and then she can clasp it to her heart forever."

July—August

Thérèse was telling me how to behave when a nun who is known to have poor judgement sets out to give me some advice—or tells me something which I know is not so. " In the first place," she said, " believe that she is well-intentioned. Then answer her very gently and, as far as possible, without being untruthful, act as though you subscribe to all that she has said."

* * *

" You are wrong," the Saint said to me, " in wanting everybody to see things your way. We desire to become like *little children*, do we not? . . . Well, little children do not know what is best for them, they think everything is good. Try to imitate them."

" Charity," Thérèse told me, quoting Saint Alphonsus Ligouri, " consists in bearing with those who are unbearable."

* * *

" The farther you advance in the spiritual life," she said, " the fewer combats will you have; or to put it better, you will be able to overcome the obstacles more easily, because you shall have learned to look on the bright side of things. It is only then that you will know how to soar above creatures and human events." It was because she had learned early in life, Thérèse told me, not to rely on the judgments of men that she found the varying opinions of creatures making little or no impression on her as death approached.

AUGUST

She said to us, " In this world, everything passes away, even *la petite Thérèse* . . . but she shall return."

AUGUST 3rd

" You are *very little*," Thérèse reminded me, " always remember that. Now when we are very little, we cannot expect to have beautiful thoughts."

AUGUST 4th

Harassed by the thought of her imminent death, I interrupted a conversation and heaving a deep sigh, I said, " I will never be able to live *sans elle* " (without her).

To make me laugh, she answered with a pun, " Therefore I shall bring you *deux ailes* " (two wings).[17]

AUGUST 5th

Referring to this passage of the Gospel; " Two women shall be grinding at the millstone, one will be taken and one will be left . . . " (Luke XVII, 35) Thérèse said: " We shall be carrying on our little traffic together, and when I see that you cannot grind the wheat all by yourself, I shall come to take you . . . ' Watch ye therefore for you do not know at what hour your Lord will come.' " (Mark XIII, 35).

Thérèse was fond of reminding me that we were two partners. It made no difference then if one had a smaller income than the other. Since we would never be separated, we would in the end be able to live on the same pension.

She was always extending herself in an effort to imbue me with her own poverty of spirit and emptiness of heart. Playfully she once reminded me, " *Bo-bonne* must remember always that she

---

[17] " *Sans elle* " and " *deux ailes* " have similar pronunciations.

is only a little domestic; she must never try to be ' une grande dame '—never! "

And one day when I had to finish the Little Hour of *None* in the Divine Office, she laughingly told me, " Go to recite *None*, and never forget that you are a very little *nonne* (nun) and the very least of all the *nonnes*."

Later when I said to her, " Then you are really going away from me? " she answered, " Oh no, not even a stone's throw away." [18]

Returning to my chief concern, I asked, " Do you really believe that I can hope to be near you in heaven? To be frank, I think this is impossible. It is as though a child with only one arm were told to fetch something from the top of a slippery pole."

Thérèse replied: " Suppose just then a great giant came along and taking the helpless little one into his arms were to swing him high in the air within reach of the desired object? . . . That is how the Heavenly Father will take care of you. But you must not become preoccupied about it at all."

All I had to do, she added, was to say to the good God, " I know I shall never be worthy of that which I hope, but I hold out my hands to Thee like a little beggar, confident that Thou wilt grant me all that I ask simply because Thou art so good."

---

[18] "Oh! pas d'une semelle." Literally, "Oh, not even a footstep away." Thérèse used this far-fetched expression to amuse Céline.

AUGUST 8th

The thought that I would have to live on without her was fast becoming a nightmare and I began to ask her repeatedly if I would soon follow her to heaven. Although she did raise my hopes for an early death, evidently when in heaven she began to judge time only in the light of eternity ! ! !

"If they write your life soon after your death," I said to her one day, " maybe I, too, by that time shall have entered eternity. Do you think this might happen? "

"Yes," she answered, "I believe that could be. But don't lose your patience about it." Then with a mischievous smile: "Be like me—see what a docile little thing I am! "

AUGUST 16th

Rising early on this morning, I found my dear little sister pale and disfigured by suffering and in great anguish.

"The demon is around me," she said, "I do not see him but I feel his presence. He is tormenting me and holds me with a grip of iron, which prevents me from getting the slightest relief. He is increasing my pain in order, I suppose, to lead me to despair."

Answering my thought, she went on plaintively, " And, I cannot pray. I can only look at the Blessed Virgin and say ' Jesus.' Oh, how necessary is that prayer at Compline—Procul recedant somnia, et noctium phantasmata." [19]

"There is something mysterious going on within me . . ."

Deeply moved, I lit a blessed candle, and the spirit of darkness fled.

AUGUST 24th

We were amusing ourselves in a kind of baby-talk which those present could not make out when Sister Saint-Stanislaus, the first Infirmarian, admiringly exclaimed:

"How precious these two young girls are with their unintelligible jargon."

Later I said to Thérèse: "Sister Saint Stanislaus is right. When we are together we are precious but I am so only when I am with you. *You* are the precious one!"

The Saint answered spiritedly, "That is why I shall come soon to take you to myself." [20]

AUGUST 24th

As she was almost gasping for breath, she kept on repeating in order to get some relief: "Je souffre, je souffre!" [21]   Soon, however, she

---

[19] "Far let idle visions fly
    No phantoms of the night molest."

[20] "que je viendrai pour vous qu'rir" (vous quierir, vous chercher).

[21] I'm suffering, I'm suffering.

began to reproach herself for moaning in this way and told me,

" Whenever I cry ' je souffre,' you must answer, ' Tant mieux.' [22] That is what I should like to say if I had the strength. So you can complete my aspiration for me."

Cost what it might, I had to obey . . . I confess, however, that I avoided the *occasion* as much as possible.

SEPTEMBER

She had been suffering much and, in order to give her a little diversion (for she always liked to look at pretty things) one of the nuns showed her an attractive little gift basket. Apparently it did not interest her, and she heaved a sigh:

" I gazed on the beauties of earth, and my soul had been dreaming of heaven."

SEPTEMBER 3rd

I had been going to and fro trying to keep order in the Infirmary, and became upset because something had gone wrong. Thérèse called, " *Bo-bonne*, no interior anxiety if you please! "

SEPTEMBER 5th

I had been jotting down on scraps of paper what had been going on between us in the

---

[22] So much the better.

Infirmary, but it was only on Sundays that there was any free time to copy these notes. This evening when I said to her,

" Today is a Sunday wasted! I have not been able to make any entries in my note book," she replied,

" That is *Lili's* opinion, but Jesus thinks differently." [23]

SEPTEMBER 11th

" You are nursing a baby," she told me, " who is very near death." Then very tenderly, " But I shall see you again, and your heart shall rejoice and your joy no man will take from you." (John XVI, 22).

And a little later; holding up her glass and reminding me of the order I had given that she must tell me what she needed, she twittered:

" Baby has a very bad taste in her mouth; please put something nice in her large glass."

SEPTEMBER 16th

Some days previously, she had been speaking to me about the necessity of mortification in the matter of answering immediately (without taking even another stitch) whenever we are summoned, either by the bell or a knock on the door.

---

[23] " C'est la mesure de Lili, mais pas celle de Jésus." If Thérèse meant " That is the measure (limitation) of Lili etc." the word " celle " would be applying the word limitation to Christ also. This is unlikely, although the sentence has been translated in this way in a foreign publication.

" I have done this all my religious life," she added, " but at the beginning, ' my house was not fully at peace '." [24]

When, on this afternoon, I was put to the test and followed her counsel promptly, she noticed it and congratulated me:

" Oh, if you only knew ! . . ." she said. " At the moment of death you will find this before you . . . This is a more glorious act than if by some skilful measures you had obtained the good will of the government for religious communities, and for ours in particular, and all France hailed you as a second Judith ! "

SEPTEMBER 23rd

Thérèse said: " You do not have to understand, you are *too little* . . ." by which she meant that I did not have to know how God is working in my soul.

SEPTEMBER 25th

She told me,

" I am going to die, that is certain. I do not know when but now it is certain."

---

[24] " Au commencement, *ma demeure* n'etait pas *pacifee* au fond de mon coeur." That is to say, " at the beginning, it was not easy going." Here the Saint borrows from Saint John of the Cross, *Cantique de l'ame strophes 1 et 2.*

I asked:

" You will look down on us from heaven won't you? " With great spontaneity, she answered, " No, *I shall come down.*"

I used to try to look in on her several times during the night, in spite of her objections. On one of the occasions, I found her with hands joined and eyes raised to heaven. " What are you doing," I asked. " You should try to get some sleep."

" I cannot," she replied, " for I am suffering too much, so I am praying."

" And what are you saying to Jesus? "

" I say nothing, I just love Him."

* * *

On one of the last days of her life, in a moment of intense suffering, she begged me:

> " Oh ! *my little Soeur Geneviève* pray for me to the Blessed Virgin. If you were sick, how I would storm heaven for you. But when it is for ourselves, we cannot be so daring."

And she sighed again: " How necessary it is to pray for the dying. If you only knew."

SEPTEMBER 28th

I remained with her the early part of this night. Several times we heard in the garden the cooing of a turtle dove, then a fluttering of wings similar to the motion of a bird which in fact suddenly alighted on the window-sill. It was truly extraordinary and it brought to mind this passage in the Canticle of Canticles:[25]

" Arise my love, my beautiful one and come, for the winter is now past; the rain is over and gone, the flowers have appeared in our land, the voice of the turtle is heard in our lands."

SEPTEMBER 30th

My dear Little Thérèse's last day of Exile

On the afternoon of this, the day of her death, Mère Agnès and I were alone with her. Trembling and exhausted, she called us to help her . . . She was in pain from head to foot. Placing one of her arms on Pauline's shoulder and the other on mine, she was able to relax for a few moments. It was then that the three o'clock bell rang. Seeing our dear little victim with her arms in the form of a cross we could only think of the Crucified Jesus; was not this little martyr His faithful image?

Her long and terrible agony began shortly after, when she could be heard repeating:

" Oh ! it is *pure* suffering because there is not a drop of consolation, no, not one.

---

[25] Cf. Cant. 11, 12.

" Oh ! my good God ! ! ! Nevertheless, I love Him, the good God . . . Oh ! my good Blessed Virgin come to my aid!

" If this is the agony, what must death be like? . . . Oh ! *ma Mère*, I assure you that the chalice is filled even to overflowing.

" Yes, my God, all that Thou dost wish but have pity on me.

" No, I would never have believed that it was possible to suffer so much . . . never, never. I can only explain it by my extreme desire to save souls.

" And tomorrow, it will probably be worse. Ah well !—so much the better."

It was heart rending to hear her as she gasped these words, in accents which, however, revealed her perfect resignation to God's Will. It was then that Mère de Gonzaga called the community. Thérèse was not able to speak but received each nun with a gracious smile. Then clasping her crucifix, she entered into the throes of a dreadful agony. Her breathing was laboured, she was drenched in a cold sweat which soon saturated her linen and the bed clothes.

She was trembling from head to foot . . . Sometime previously, Thérèse had said to us:

" My dear little Sisters [26] please don't be distressed if my parting farewell is not directed to any one of you. Just what will happen at

---

[26] Pauline, Marie, and Céline.

the last moment is in God's Hands, of course.
If He leaves the choice to me, however, my
final adieu will be for our Mother [27] because she
is my Prioress."

On this evening of her death, therefore, as I
placed a small piece of ice on Thérèse's parched
lips, I received in return a beautiful smile. As
she fixed a tender gaze on me, it seemed that she
was looking into the future, with all that it held
for me. Her superhuman expression was full of
encouragement and promise as though she were
saying to me:

" Va, va, ma Céline, je serais avec toi . . . " [28]

Was this Our Lord's way of consoling me for the
long, laborious course which, on Thérèse's
account, I was still to run on this earth? I do
not know, but I can say that the remembrance
of this last farewell, so ardently desired by all
yet reserved for me alone, has been for me a
tower of spiritual strength for the past fifty-five
years . . .

Believing that Soeur Thérèse's parting adieu
had been not for our Mother but for me, the
community was startled. But a moment later,
the Saint's half-veiled eyes, agonizing once more,
travelled until they met those of Mère de Gonzague, who was kneeling at her side.

---

[27] Mère de Gonzague.
[28] " Go on with courage, my Céline; I shall be with you."

The latter, believing that the agony would be prolonged, dismissed the community and the angelic patient turning to her, asked

"*Ma Mère*, isn't this the agony? Am I not going to die?"

On the response that God might wish to extend the time of her suffering, Thérèse sighed in a sweet and plaintive voice:

"Eh bien ! . . . allons, allons ! . . . Oh ! je ne voudrais pas moins souffrir ! " [29]

Then gazing on her Crucifix:

"Oh ! . . . Je L'aime ! . . . Mon Dieu, je . . . vous . . . aime ! ! ! " [30]

These were her last words. Hardly had she uttered them when, to our great surprise, she sank down on the pillow with her head a little to the right. Then suddenly, she raised herself up as though called by some mysterious voice, opened her eyes and fixed a radiant gaze on a spot a little above the miraculous statue of Our Lady of the Smile. Thérèse remained in this position for some moments, about the time required to recite a Credo slowly.

Often during life I have tried to analyze this ecstatic gaze which was certainly something more

---

[29] "Oh well ! So be it, so be it. No, I would not want to suffer less."

[30] "Oh ! . . . I love Him ! . . . My God, I . . . love . . Thee ! "

than a simple reflection of eternal beatitude. I have reached the following conclusions which I humbly submit to the reader.

At first, her expression had an air of *confident assurance* combined with a *joyful attitude of expectancy*: as the story of her soul unfolded, she might have been asking God what He thought of it.

And when she had His answer her expression changed to one of *profound astonishment and then to overflowing gratitude*.

I have always liked to believe that we were privileged to assist at Thérèse's Judgment. She had on the one hand been found worthy to appear *Debout* [31] before the Son of Man; on the other hand, she was, as it were, overcome by the realization of her bewildering reward, a glory which "infinitely surpasses my boundless desires." [32] This caused her whole being, I thought, to vibrate under the weight of so much love and in spite of her effort to withstand the continuous assault, she finally succumbed, closed her eyes and died. It was September 30, 1897, at seven-twenty in the evening.

* * *

Submerged in grief, I fled from the Infirmary and went outdoors. In my naïvete, I was really

[31] *Standing*—Cf. Luke XXI, 36.
[32] Cf. Letter to Mère Agnès, May 28, 1897.

hoping to catch a glimpse of her in the heavens but as it was raining, the sky was completely overcast. Leaning against the column of one of the cloisters I began to sob. If only the stars would come out, I thought to myself. Almost immediately, the clouds dispersed and stars were soon studding the sky.

On the return journey home, my uncle and aunt [33] who had been praying in the outer chapel during Thérèse's agony, were also struck by this sudden change of weather which enabled them so unexpectedly to close their umbrellas.

THE LAST TEAR OF SAINT THÉRÈSE

After the Saint's death, when the community had dispersed and I found myself alone with Thérèse, I noticed that a tear was still shining on her eyelid. I longed to preserve it.

In the absence of something better, I hastily removed the tear with the corner of a coarse white handkerchief, tore away the precious strip, and then hemmed it up again. In this way, I would not call attention to the fact that I had saved this precious trophy of Thérèse's final combat.

I took great care to preserve this piece of cloth which retained a very *definite imprint* of the spot moistened by the memorable tear. Years later, it was cut out in the shape of a tear and,

---

[33] Isidore and Céline Guérin.

surrounded by diamonds, placed in a reliquary, in the form of a massive bronze angel in armour.

A REFLECTION OF ETERNAL BEATITUDE

In her sleep of death, on Thérèse's countenance there was a reflection of eternal happiness and a celestial smile. That which struck me most, however, was a certain vitality and joy with which her eyelids (tightly closed) seemed to vibrate. Death was forgotten while this consolation lasted. I might add that in all my contacts with our Sisters who have died since then, I have never noticed anything like it.

Since Thérèse was so beautiful in death, I tried to take her picture before she was carried from the Infirmary to the choir on October 1, 1897. Because of various handicaps, I was not very successful, although her heavenly smile did come through. Moreover, her features which had not as yet undergone any change, could be clearly distinguished in this first picture.

I took another photograph on Sunday, October 3, in the afternoon while she lay exposed on her flowery bier in the choir. But this picture showed her features to be elongated and, curiously, her blond eyebrows were dark brown —almost black. She was still majestic but we could no longer recognize her.

It was for this reason that in 1905, at the urgent request of the community I painted a picture of Thérèse as she had appeared immediately after death. For model, I used the first picture taken in the Infirmary on October 1, 1897. The Sisters who had been her contemporaries considered my portrait a perfect likeness of our Saint. It was this picture which was published in all editions of *Histoire d'une Ame*, after the year 1906.

The picture taken on October 3, 1897, had appeared in the preceding editions only because we had nothing better to offer. But in order to make it presentable, some retouches had been necessary.

INSCRIPTION ON THE CROSS OVER
SOEUR THÉRÈSE'S GRAVE

On October 4, 1897, Soeur Thérèse was buried in the first grave of our newly enclosed plot in the municipal cemetery of Lisieux. Mère Agnès had printed on the wooden cross destined for her tomb:

Soeur Thérèse de l'Enfant Jésus 1873—1897
with these lines from the Saint's poem Rappelle-Toi:

> Que je veux, o mon Dieu
> Porter loin ton feu
> Rappelle-Toi.[34]

---

[34] How I long, O my Radiant Star
To scatter Thy Beams afar,
Remember Thou.

This inscription was almost entirely effaced when a workman took hold of the cross while the paint was still wet. Mère Agnès considered this an indication of God's will, and inscribed on the cross instead Thérèse's prophecy:

JE VEUX PASSER MON CIEL A FAIRE DU BIEN SUR LA TERRE.[35]

---

[35] "I will spend my heaven doing good on earth." At the outset, my sister had desired to use this quotation but had hesitated in the name of prudence.

APPENDIX

From the Letters of Approbation for the French edition: *Conseils et Souvenirs.*

" . . . It was with great edification and deep emotion that I read this *Memoir* which, completing, so to speak, the *Autobiography*, delineates the spiritual portrait of Saint Thérèse. . . . The characteristic features of her moral profile which certain writers have tried to alter by their arbitrary interpretations, are seen in their true light in these pages . . .

" Once more, let me thank Soeur Geneviève and the Carmel of Lisieux, that Carmel which is the *faithful guardian of a unique spirit of sanctity and of a Way which is illuminating a world of souls.*

ADEODATUS CARDINAL PIAZZA, O.C.D.,
(*Secretary of the Sacred Congregation of the Consistorial*).

Rome, January 31, 1953.

" . . . This *Memoir* proves that sanctity does not consist in words nor in any particular norm of external behaviour. Rather, it has its origin in that love which the Holy Spirit of God sheds abroad in souls. Such love, for the most part hidden while in silence it is transforming the souls, betrays itself not only in the practice of virtue but likewise by the efficacy of its works.

" Yet, from another standpoint, we may still maintain that this love remains concealed because there is, apparently, no struggle in the practice of virtue and also by reason of the humble simplicity of the souls attitudes and reactions. Simplicity in itself is an elusive thing which cannot be explained or defined; we must see it in operation if we are to know it for what it is. This *Memoir* gives us a comprehensive picture of this grace of simplicity in full swing in the life of Saint Thérèse of the Child Jesus. . . . "

> PÈRE MARIE-EUGÉNE, O.C.D.,
> (*First Definitor General*).

December 3, 1952.

" Even the most casual reader of Saint Thérèse's *Autobiography* could not fail to note and be impressed by the strong bond of love which existed between Thérèse Martin and her sister Céline. This *Memoir*, therefore, needs no further introduction . . .

" The lessons Thérèse gives us in these pages . . . resemble in a certain way the pattern of the Gospel narratives. The Saint comes to life, as it were, and in the rôle of a big sister, she receives her sister's confidences, answers her questions . . . and strives to regulate the disturbed emotion.

" Because the Mother Prioress reserved to herself the formal training of the novitiate, . . . Thérèse was free to lead the novices according to the interior promptings of her own enlightened soul. That is why today we find Thérèse of the Child Jesus encouragingly reminding us through these spiritual contacts with the young sisters that God will assuredly perfect His admirable designs of love in our souls, if He finds us humble, interiorly poor, and possessed of a daring confidence. This was the theme underlying all Thérèse's teaching. . . .

" It has been said that all that we may learn about the saints, each new maxim or saying of theirs authentically recorded, takes on the importance of a message sent down to us by the Holy Spirit. Nor can we adequately judge its possible impact on souls in our own day or in the generations to come. When there is question of Saint Thérèse of Lisieux, however, and her unique spiritual power over all hearts, can we fully assess the importance of this book with its wide range of reminiscences? . . . "

Père Elisée de la Nativité, O.C.D.
Paris, May 8, 1952.

THOUGHTS OF ST. THÉRÈSE

No. 0217. 180 Pp.
PB. Imprimatur.

6.00

Composed of 328 brief quotations arranged under 20 different topics, such as love of God, love of neighbor, faith, humility, confidence, self-abandonment, gratitude, zeal and suffering, *Thoughts of St. Thérèse* consists of the Saint's own words and writings—from *The Story of a Soul* (her autobiography), *Counsels and Reminiscences*, and her letters.

This book shows St. Thérèse's greatness of soul and that she was no Saint by accident. Beautiful and surprising! A book cherished by many.

ST. THÉRÈSE, THE LITTLE FLOWER
—The Making of a Saint—
By John Beevers

What factors conspired to shape St. Thérèse of the Child Jesus? John Beevers addresses himself to this question in this book. He concentrates on St. Thérèse's childhood and youth and shows how her life is a miracle of divine grace and an example of the spiritual greatness that can be achieved by perfect love of God.

No. 0181. 157 Pp. PB.

6.00

Children's Books on St. Thérèse . . .

THE LITTLE FLOWER

By Mary Fabyan Windeatt

No. 1139. 167 Pp.
PB. Imprimatur.

8.00

The Story of St. Thérèse of the Child Jesus. The story of St. Thérèse, for children 10 and up, and of her "Little Way of Spiritual Childhood," whereby she would say "Yes" to whatever Our Lord asked of her, and how she thereby became a great Saint.

CATHOLIC CHILDREN'S TREASURE BOX. *Stories, Poems, Games, Fun Things to Make and Do.* Books 1-10. Maryknoll Sisters (1950's). Wonderful full-color series combining fun, innocence and Catholic faith! These books <u>teach children to love God and their holy Catholic Faith and show them how to be good</u>! Stories include "A Little Girl Named Thérèse" (St. Thérèse—Bks. 1-6), Wupsy (a Guardian Angel), "The Boy Who Told Lies," etc. For a wide range of ages (Pre-School thru about 10). Children love them! Beautiful pictures!

No. 1371 (Set). 32 pp. ea. PB. Imprimatur.
10¼" x 8¼". Full color on every page.
$4.50 each. Set of all 10—$35.00

If you have enjoyed this book, consider making your next selection from among the following . . .

At your Bookdealer or direct from the Publisher.
Call Toll Free 1-800-437-5876

ABOUT THE AUTHOR

Sister Geneviève of the Holy Face (Celine Martin), born April 28, 1869, was the second to the youngest of the five Martin sisters and the last one to enter the religious life. She was St. Thérèse's childhood confidant and later in the Carmel of Lisieux her spiritual disciple. It is to Sister Geneviève that we owe not only this present volume on St. Thérèse, but also many of the photographs we have of the Saint, as well as the famous portraits of St. Thérèse which she painted.

Sister Geneviève outlived all her sisters. She died in 1959, having spent more than 64 years in Carmel.